The Chomolungma Diaries

Climbing Mount Everest with a commercial expedition

MARK HORRELL

Published by Mountain Footsteps Press

Copyright © 2016 Mark Horrell
www.markhorrell.com
All rights reserved

First published as an ebook 2012
Revised edition published 2016

ISBN (paperback): 978-0-9934130-4-9
ISBN (ebook): 978-0-9934130-3-2

"If I am asked: what is the use of climbing this highest mountain? I reply, No use at all; no more than kicking a football about or dancing or playing on the piano ... But if there is no use, there is unquestionably good in climbing Mount Everest. The accomplishment of such a feat will elevate the human spirit."

Francis Younghusband

THE
CHOMOLUNGMA
DIARIES

DAY 1
THE ONLY WAY TO ACCLIMATISE IN A DIRTY
OLD TOWN

Wednesday, 11th of April 2012 – Nyalam, Tibet

There are nicer places to spend the first day of an expedition than Nyalam, about an hour up the Friendship Highway from Zhangmu on the Chinese-Nepalese border.

Perched on a hill, the town comprises a single curved main street lined with concrete buildings and red-curtained doorways. It's cold and damp, and a grey mist hangs in the air – air that's already thin because the altitude here is 3,500m. Wood smoke drifts from doorways and mixes with the mist, and the atmosphere is unpleasant. Streams of dirty water rush down the hill on each side of the street. Dark brown hills rise above a town which sits high above a deep river gorge, a continuation of the Bhote Khosi River which we followed up from Nepal yesterday.

A thin layer of snow has dusted the hills, and sleet is falling this morning. It's quite a culture shock from Kathmandu, where we spent the previous day. A noisy storm kept us awake as it battered the shutters of the hotel windows the night before we left, sending a solar panel clattering to the ground from a rooftop nearby, but otherwise Kathmandu had been warm and pleasant. Here in Nyalam it's grey and dull, and much colder than any of us expected. There's no real reason to stop for a night here, except to acclimatise. Although only an hour's drive away, the border town of Zhangmu is much lower at 2,300m, so not much would be gained by staying there; while the next town – Tingri at 4,300m – is too high for people not yet accustomed to the altitude.

Only last week Tibet was closed to visitors. As soon as the Chinese government opened the border there was a flurry of people applying for visas. We got ours on Monday and travelled up yesterday. Consequently everyone is here at the same time: climbers on their way to Shishapangma, Cho Oyu, and Everest like ourselves; and trekkers bound for Advanced Base Camp to coincide with the big expeditions. To add to the congestion we're all eating in the same restaurant owned by the China Tibet Mountaineering Association (CTMA), who are providing all our meals, accommodation and transport while we travel through Tibet. We have breakfast, lunch and dinner in a small room up a grubby stepladder, and have to wait for other teams to finish before we can get a table.

After lunch Ian and I find a much nicer bar up the hill, accurately if unimaginatively named the Base Camp Western Food and Coffee Bar, where we have a coffee and escape the snow while wandering the town in the morning. We like it enough that we decide to return with our friends in the afternoon. I'm here with Mark Dickson and Ian Cartwright, whom I've climbed with on many previous expeditions, most recently Manaslu in Nepal; and Phil Crampton, who was our expedition leader on Manaslu and again here on Everest. We're joined by Grant 'Axe' Rawlinson, a compact New Zealander who reached 8,300m on Everest last year and has come back for a second attempt.

Opinion is divided on whether drinking beer in a bar is a sensible way to spend an afternoon while you're still acclimatising. On the one hand it's important to keep hydrated, but drinking to excess can actually have a detrimental effect. While Phil and I drink from thimble-sized glasses to moderate our intake, Ian and Mark go at it like the clappers. I noticed on Manaslu they bear a passing resemblance to Laurel and Hardy during a hard drinking session, with a tall, thin, quiet one who is always getting blamed for the nice mess the pair of them keep getting into, and a short, stocky, boisterous one who is always leading the way but denying responsibility for it. Mark keeps calling for more beer and Ian keeps saying yes.

We only met Grant a couple of days ago, but already Mark is wasting no time in getting to know him better.

'So why do they call you "Axe", Grant – is it because of the size of your chopper?'

'When I played rugby I was a scrum half, and I tackled hard and low,' Grant replies.

Scrum halves have a reputation for being small and garrulous, and Grant appears to have both these qualities. Mark played rugby too, so I expect they'll get along.

I sip in quiet witness while Phil, who as expedition leader should be taking more care of us, really isn't helping much.

'It's good you guys are keeping yourselves hydrated,' he says.

Ian is a likeable character who reached the summit of Manaslu last year before giving his oxygen to another climber who was in difficulty on the way down. It was an act which said much about him as a person: generous to a fault, even when his decisions aren't that wise. Manaslu was his first 8,000m summit, and without his oxygen he might have had trouble himself.

'We'll have plenty of oxygen available on Everest,' Phil says, 'and there should be no reason for any of you to give yours away.'

Mark grins. 'Ian will be setting up a gazebo with his bottles on the North Col. He'll be shouting at passing climbers: "come and get it, free oxygen".'

Phil is something of an unsung hero too. We talk about Lincoln Hall, a climber who died of cancer a couple of weeks ago. He was famous for collapsing just below the summit of Everest in 2006 and being left for dead, but he survived the night and was found alive the following morning. He lived to tell the tale. Phil was part of the team who found him, but he was suffering from frostbite. Instead of waiting for Lincoln Hall to recover, like the other climbers in the team, Phil returned to Camp 3 to rouse Sherpas to help with oxygen. While the other climbers involved in the rescue have justifiably received a great deal of publicity and praise for their part in it, Phil's role has been largely forgotten. But this is typical of him. As owner of the high-altitude mountaineering company Altitude Junkies he might have made publicity out of our rescue of the climber on Manaslu, involving four members of his team, but he chose to say nothing. Ian wasn't so lucky – I blogged about it myself because I felt he deserved some credit.

By the time we leave for dinner there are fourteen large Lhasa Beer bottles on the table, although we've diluted them with pakoras, chips, coffee and yak balls (these are balls made of yak meat, rather than what you're thinking). Back at the restaurant more teams have arrived and there are people waiting outside. Nobody is eating at the bar up the road, even though the food is better, because we've all paid the CTMA to travel in Tibet, and our meals are included.

It's going to be worse at breakfast; Phil is even thinking of leaving early and having breakfast in Tingri. Our sirdar Dorje talks him out of it, and after another greasy Chinese meal we turn in for bed.

Our hotel does nothing to raise Nyalam's standing. Although the rooms are comfortable enough, there's no running water. We brush our teeth with mineral water and flush the toilet with pans filled from a butt outside the door. We'll be waiting to reach Everest Base Camp before we shower again.

DAY 2
EVEREST FROM THE TIBETAN PLATEAU

Thursday, 12th of April 2012 – Tingri, Tibet

Our Russian team member Mila is a bit more perky at breakfast this morning. She's been feeling under the weather these last few days and Phil is convinced it's been stress-related. While the rest of us have tourist visas for Nepal, Mila has a business visa, and this was a problem when it came for us to apply for visas for Tibet. At one point it seemed that none of us would be able to get into Tibet because of the need to travel on a group visa. Through a combination of diplomacy, paperwork and payment this was resolved.

Then there was the worry of her 'dharma book'. It's wise not to carry anything into Tibet supportive of the Dalai Lama or critical of the Chinese government because all bags are searched rigorously at the border. Any items deemed offensive are confiscated, and in the worst cases entry is refused. Mila has a big blue book of Buddhism that she wants to read at Base Camp, and she was worried the Chinese border guards might consider it subversive literature and refuse entry to us all. The guard opened it up and read a few paragraphs before handing it back to her and waving her through.

By yesterday evening it was evident that Mila's worries had evaporated into the thin Tibetan air, and all of us would be making it to Base Camp safely to begin our attempt on the mountain.

At breakfast there are still lots of people queuing for tables and waiting to pounce as soon as one is vacated. I seem to be a slower eater than the rest of the team and am still finishing my last few mouthfuls of Tibetan bread and marmalade when everyone else gets up to leave. I'm immediately engulfed by a party of half a dozen mixed Europeans as I remain in my seat, chewing frantically and trying to wash it down with a few swigs of jasmine tea.

We leave in a minibus at 9.45am China time. This is slightly confusing. Because China time is set thousands of miles east in Beijing, many people here remain on the more appropriate Nepalese time zone which is two hours and fifteen minutes behind.

The sky is much clearer this morning, and the conditions are a complete contrast to the damp misty sleet of yesterday. The road continues up the valley into an arid desert landscape, and I regret leaving my sunglasses in my bag as the sun cuts through the thin high-altitude air. We pass clusters of traditional whitewashed Tibetan houses. These sit within walled compounds, and piles of yak dung and firewood dry on flat roofs.

At the top of the valley the road rises in a series of zigzags onto the Tibetan plateau. We reach a pass, the Tong La at 5,120m, and stop for photos of a classic Tibetan landscape. Prayer flags and prayer wheels bedeck the pass and to the north the land stretches endlessly across a desert plain. To the south a ragged chain of snow-capped mountains rises above the border with Nepal, and to the west is the solitary giant of Shishapangma, one of the world's fourteen 8,000m peaks, and the only one wholly in China. Today its wall of ice stands wreathed in its own personal cloud, but it's still the best view I've had of it, having passed this way twice before.

We continue onwards and cross another high pass before descending 600m. An hour later we get our first view of Everest straight in front of us, with its black pyramid leaping in a steep wall 4,000m above the plateau. From the south in Nepal, where other huge snow-capped mountains surround it, views of

6

Everest are less dramatic and its supremacy is less obvious. But from the northern side our views are mainly of brown hills and it's easy to believe that I'm looking at the highest mountain on Earth.

On the skyline to its right are Gyachung Kang and Cho Oyu, two more of the world's highest mountains. They are more heavily snow capped than Everest but less prominent, huge sprawling massifs wreathed in cloud. Everest is a lofty perch towering above the horizon, the North-East Ridge slowly rising up to join the summit pyramid, from which a rock wall drops away sharply to the south. Features such as the North Ridge and Norton Couloir are prominent on its northern face. Murderous jet-stream winds pound its summit and blast a huge plume of cloud off the length of the North-East Ridge and beyond. I think it's the blackness which is most forbidding, a combination of its steepness and the jet-stream winds which give snow little chance to accumulate.

It's impossible to believe that in a few short weeks we might be tiny figures creeping towards the summit, but there's still a long way to go before we find ourselves in that position, if at all. More easy to credit is why Sherpas believe this place to be the abode of mountain gods at whose mercy you may be permitted to tread its slopes. Today it would be impossible. Only when the winds vanish and the plume melts away will permission be granted, and that's something no human power can control, not even the Chinese.

The billiard-table smooth tarmac of the Friendship Highway, which was resurfaced all the way from Lhasa in time for the Beijing Olympics in 2008, enables us to reach Tingri in around three hours. It's a different world to Nyalam here. From a damp misty gorge we find ourselves on a dusty plateau surrounded by brown hills. Although the sun is fierce we're at 4,300m and it's hardly warm. Tingri is a single street which, but for its whitewashed Tibetan houses, could be straight out of the Wild West.

We check in to the amusingly named Ha Hoo Hotel in a little walled compound on the eastern end of town. It's one of the few places which is clean enough for westerners and our delicate western stomachs, so I've actually had lunch here twice before on previous expeditions. As with the hotel in Nyalam, the rooms are clean but the toilets are grim, and again there's no running water.

We arrive in time for lunch: a big bowl of rice and a series of Chinese dishes to share in succession until nobody round the table can take any more. Standard fare when travelling in China. All restaurants have round tables with a revolving tray in the middle to rotate dishes around (which Phil calls a 'lazy Susan'). They are providing us with Lhasa Beer to go with every meal, but I'm a bit concerned because Mark has stopped drinking. This suggests something must be wrong.

In the afternoon we get some exercise by strolling up the wide dusty main street. I walk with Grant, and he tells me about his attempt on Everest last year, also from the north side.

'Our summit day was a bit of a disaster. The straps of my crampons were so frozen that it took an age to tie them, and by the time I managed it my fingers were so cold. Then I broke my snow goggles trying to put them on, so I started out with no goggles. I walked about fifty metres out of camp into the teeth of a gale. "Fuck this," I thought to myself, and headed back to my tent for the wind to die down, but it just got worse, so that was that. It wasn't the right summit weather and the winds hadn't been forecast. Our expedition leader was going up ahead trying to get everyone to turn back. Only one of our team summited, and he said his Sherpa was doing everything for him, clipping him into all the ropes. When he got to the summit the cornea in one of his eyes froze and he had to descend half-blind. His Sherpa was doing each rappel with him and the pair of them were tied together. Eventually they got far enough down that his cornea thawed and he was able to descend by himself. I don't want to get to the summit like that, you know. I want to get up and down by myself.'

I agree with Grant, but you don't always know what it's going to be like when you get up there. If I find myself struggling then I'm sure I will accept every little bit of help my

Sherpa, Chongba, can provide, as I did on Manaslu.

A cold wind whistles across the plateau and whips up the dust into our faces. Up ahead of us Mark and Ian have turned around and are coming back.

'Fuck this!' Mark says. We head back to the hotel.

Phil has a few logistical difficulties at dinner time. He was hoping to send the truck with all our equipment and a bus with all the Sherpas to Base Camp tomorrow, so that everything is ready when we arrive the following day. But all the buses are busy ferrying other teams between Nyalam and Tingri, and only four people are allowed in each truck. Four Sherpas to unload seven tons of equipment and set up camp is asking a bit much, so he thinks he will have to charter another vehicle to take some of the Sherpas – but this takes time and is expensive. It means we'll have to wait for some of the facilities to be set up after we arrive.

We tell him that we don't mind. Not everybody has Sherpas working hard to set up camp for them. We are in no hurry. We can relax and acclimatise, drinking tea as we wait for our team to build the camp around us. It's a luxury we don't take for granted.

DAY 3
ONE OF THE WORLD'S GREAT VIEWS

Friday, 13th of April 2012 – Tingri, Tibet

I have a disconcerting experience when I go to the toilet after breakfast this morning. It's a standard Tibetan long-drop where you crap through a hole in the floor into a deep pit. Halfway through, I catch a glimpse of movement beneath me and look down to see a cow moving around there. It's too late to do anything about it and I have no choice but to continue what I'm doing. Happily the cow doesn't seem to mind.

It's a fine cloudless morning in Tingri and the winds are light, so most of us head up to the viewpoint for a spot of light acclimatisation. A few hundred yards down the main street, a concrete track leads off up a small hill with a radio mast. It's an easy walk and one of the world's classic views greets me at the top. Across a grassy plateau Everest's dark pyramid and the white massifs of Gyachung Kang and Cho Oyu line up across the horizon. Lots of climbers are mingling at the top of the hill and chatting loudly, so I walk a little away from them to have this moment to myself. Unfortunately there are houses at the foot of the hill, and someone keeps driving up and down the road in a noisy petrol-driven cart. Occasionally the engine is turned off and I'm able to contemplate the view in silence. It's one I'm unlikely to forget and I feel very lucky.

Conversation is quite intense at lunchtime back at the Ha Hoo Hotel. The final member of our group is Margaret Watroba, a 62-year-old Australian who was originally a Polish immigrant who fled her country during the Communist years. A couple of days ago I had a conversation with her about the physical attributes of footballers which included a discussion of David Beckham modelling in his underpants (she started it, not me). Until now Margaret's conversation has been quite light-hearted, but today it's a little deeper. She tells us about how she fled Poland with her husband in 1980.

'I told my mother I was going on holiday to Austria, and when we got there we sought asylum in a refugee camp, and eventually emigrated to Australia. When I said goodbye to my mother I held her so tightly; I didn't know if I would see her again. "But I will see you next week," she said to me, but I couldn't tell her what I was going to do. In the end I saw her only once more, ten years later, before she died.'

Margaret climbed Everest from the south side with Phil last year, and Manaslu a couple of years earlier. I don't expect I'll be able to keep up with her.

If this isn't enough profundity for one day, Mila chips in with some of her own. She tells me about a 60-year-old Russian priest who is planning to carry a cross to the summit.

'What, like Jesus?' I say.

'I think it's his Sherpa who will be carrying the cross,' she replies.

'Well, as long as he takes it back down and gives his Sherpa a good bonus, I don't see a problem.'

'I think he's intending to leave it there.'

'But that's disgusting – that's litter!'

For a second I'm worried I've said something offensive, but it turns out that Mila has even stronger feelings.

'I find it in very poor taste. If it's true then I will try to sabotage it.'

I'm sure she's not alone. Sherpas consider Everest to be the abode of mountain gods. They won't set foot on it until they've conducted a puja ceremony to appease them. It's hard to believe they will allow this priest to succeed in his attempt to turn it into a Christian mountain. Many mountains in South America have crosses on the summit, but not here in the Himalayas, a world of Buddhists and Hindus. As Mila says, it would be in poor taste.

DAY 4
THE EVEREST SHORTCUT

Saturday, 14th of April 2012 – Base Camp, Everest, Tibet

We have an interesting drive to Everest Base Camp this morning, leaving from Tingri at 4.15am Nepali time. There are two routes to Everest from here. To the east the main highway is tarmacked most of the way and an easy drive for buses, while to the west a dirt track heads off to Cho Oyu Base Camp. In between, the scenic route to Everest crosses streams and passes, and is normally only accessible to Land Cruisers.

The driver of our big battle bus opts for the latter, confident he can get through, but we soon begin to suspect he doesn't know the way. First a barrier is down across the road and he tries to take a diversion round it across rough earth, but gets lost. One of our Sherpas, Ang Gelu, jumps out and shines his head torch across the rough ground to search for a feasible route, much to the amusement of everyone on board – everyone except Phil, that is, who is keen to get to Base Camp early, as there's much work to be done when we arrive. Eventually we're able to rouse an official to let us through the barrier, but then, keen to make up for lost time, our driver starts hurtling up the road to Cho Oyu and misses the turn to Everest. Luckily Ang Gelu is alert, and we reverse back onto the right road.

The road is spectacular once the sun comes up, but there are moments when we wonder if the bus is going to make it. We pass along narrow tracks high above icy rivers and drop down again. All the while snow-capped peaks are visible across a dusty plateau flecked with green. We cross sheets of ice and drive carefully across frozen fords. Then we rise up to a gentle pass and drop down again, and Everest is visible at an unusual angle on the horizon beyond – at least, four Sherpas and Phil, who have all climbed Everest multiple times, are convinced it's Everest with its black rock pyramid towering over the other mountains on the horizon. We can't quite identify the features on the summit pyramid from this unusual angle, and surprisingly the mountain is devoid of its telltale plume of cloud as jet-stream winds bash its summit, but nobody seems to have any doubt the mountain we're looking at can be anything other than Everest.

Mark notices another big mountain wreathed in cloud further to the right, which he photographs, but he decides not to say anything. I take several photos of the clear black pyramid and some video footage to go with it. It's only when we drop down onto the main highway and begin our ascent up the Rongbuk Valley, with Everest dominating the view ahead of us, that we discover a large lenticular cloud hanging over its slopes all the way down to the North Col. For it to have descended so quickly, a perfect summit day must have turned into a hellish nightmare in a matter of minutes. It becomes clear we've been looking at the wrong mountain, and the clear black pyramid we thought was Everest was most probably Makalu.

We've made good time, and arrive at Base Camp at 8.00am Nepali time (which will now be the time zone we work to throughout the expedition). It's a huge flat rocky area beyond the terminal moraine of the Rongbuk Glacier. Although there are small rocky hills on either side, some of which have sorry-looking glaciers spilling down from them, Everest screams for attention up ahead and nothing else matters. It rises nearly four vertical kilometres above us, and its North Face and North-East Ridge can be seen in their entirety from here. Today, wrapped in horizontal layers of lenticular cloud like a heavy chain tied around its body, it looks frightening.

Only on certain days is the weather sedate enough for it to be climbable, and identifying one of those days is key for us once we're acclimatised, exercised and rested. Not everyone succeeds in identifying this weather window. When they don't the stories can become the disaster tales of Everest legend, recited in books which sell in their millions and give the mountain its fearsome reputation.

With eight Sherpas and six kitchen staff to help him, Phil insists that none of us paying clients should help out with all the hard work still to be done today. It's better, he says, for us to rest and acclimatise since we've jumped from 4,300m at Tingri to 5,160m here, and have reached this altitude in only five days. Chedar and the other Sherpas who arrived yesterday have already put up three of the big yellow storage and kitchen tents, and we sit in one of them drinking tea while the boys work around us.

Twice we're called out to help with the big Mountain Hardwear dome tents as they flap in the wind, but for the remainder of the time we laze around. By the end of the afternoon Phil and the Sherpas have worked like Trojans. Six yellow kitchen and storage tents have been erected, two dome tents, and twelve comfy three-man sleeping tents. Tomorrow all they have left to do is complete setting up the recreation dome and pitch two toilet-cum-shower tents. It's going to be a luxurious base camp.

In the evening I reacquaint myself with the dining dome that we ate in on Manaslu. It's a bit more spacious this time, with only seven of us inside compared with the eleven we had on Manaslu, but the kitchen sink with the hot water, the heaters and the comfy director's chairs mean it will be far more comfortable to dine here than any of the places we ate at in Nyalam and Tingri.

Phil tells us many people have been visiting throughout the day: friends of the Sherpas, and Crazy Chris, leader of the Adventure Peaks expedition team, one of the few other teams here already. I've met him a couple of times before, at Concordia in the Pakistan Karakoram in 2009 when he 'escorted' the top woman climber Gerlinde Kaltenbrunner down the easier trail to Askole while the group he was leading took the rather more strenuous high route over the Gondokoro La. I gave him the nickname Crazy Chris after a story he told me in Sam's Bar the following year about an unusual night out in Kathmandu, which unfortunately cannot be repeated here for reasons of taste.

Phil tells us some of his former students from the Tibetan mountaineering school in Lhasa, where he used to work, have visited.

'These dudes were speaking fluent English,' he says, 'and they learned it from me. It made me feel proud.'

'Well, to be fair, if they were speaking fluent English then they can't have learned it from you,' Mark says.

'What were they saying?' Grant asks. '"Fuck, yeah, fucking shit, fuck, yeah", "can you say anything else?", "Fuck no!"'

It's debatable whether Grant's own use of English is any less colourful than Phil's, but this outburst has us in stitches anyway.

I have a mild headache tonight, and my stomach is feeling a little delicate after our big jump in altitude, but this is normal and nothing to be concerned about. We have plenty of rest days ahead of us here at Base Camp for me to get acclimatised. I'm glad when we turn in for the night at eight o'clock, although my sleep is interrupted.

DAY 5
BASE CAMP COMMUNICATIONS

Sunday, 15th of April 2012 – Base Camp, Everest, Tibet

Our first full day at Base Camp is a day of mixed successes. In the morning Phil sets up the first part of the 'recreation dome', which turns out to be a giant white sheet covering an entire wall for projecting movies onto. He's very proud of it and calls me over to come and take a look. It's enormous.

'It's like an IMAX theatre,' I remark. 'We're going to have to watch Dorje's Everest film on it.'

Our sirdar Dorje is famous for being one of the Sherpas who carried David Breashears's giant IMAX video camera to the summit of Everest for the Everest IMAX film in 1996, a few days after the disaster described in Jon Krakauer's Everest bestseller *Into Thin Air*. Unfortunately the cinema requires the petrol-driven generator to be running rather than the solar panels. Even with the combined brains of three engineers (Ian, Grant and Margaret) we can't get it working (I say 'we', but my role involves making frivolous remarks while they fiddle around).

A bigger problem for me is the internet connection. We're intending to use the same BGAN/Inmarsat satellite system that we used on Manaslu for internet access. Phil takes it to several locations around Base Camp but can't get a signal anywhere. He suspects the Chinese government may be blocking it so that people can't blog anything negative about Tibet. He goes to talk to other teams and they all confirm their BGANs aren't working either.

Then there appears to be a lifeline. Chris from the Adventure Peaks team says he was able to get a signal from a small hillside above camp, so Phil decides to go and check it out. I watch him scramble up a gully of boulders and cross a small glacier. Twice he falls over and he later tells me he used his rugged laptop case to arrest. After about fifteen minutes of climbing he finds the place where Chris has built a wall to hide behind, and he stops to check for a signal. If it works then we'll be able to prepare our blogs down at Base Camp; Phil will climb up the hill each day to send them for us.

But there's nothing. It later emerges Chris isn't using BGAN but another system. It will be disappointing if we can't use the BGAN to send blog posts and emails, but most of us are getting a 3G connection on our iPhones and Blackberries, so tomorrow we'll look for a different solution using these while Phil keeps trying to get the BGAN working. On the plus side I discover I can get free internet access for web browsing using my Kindle. Although it's not a great user experience – web speak for a pain in the backside – it means I can check a lot of things I didn't think I'd be able to.

In the evening our cook Da Pasang and assistant cook Pemba make us the most delicious chicken sizzlers. They arrive on hot plates, and we enjoy a couple of glasses of red wine with them. Although my appetite isn't perfect yet as I adjust to our 5,160m altitude, this goes down very easily. The downside to dinner tonight is when we discover that Grant is a mine of bad jokes. Most of them have been around since the 1950s and have embellished many a Christmas cracker. Hopefully the joke mine will be fully excavated by tomorrow lunchtime, and the mine-workers will receive their marching orders.

DAY 6
BASE CAMP IT SUPPORT AND CINEMA HELL

Monday, 16th of April 2012 – Base Camp, Everest, Tibet

It's beautiful cloudless weather this morning and Everest is clear. Jet-stream winds linger on the summit and the mountain is adorned with its distinctive plume of cloud, flowing off the North-East Ridge like a cape and reminding me that to the Sherpas Everest is a living being, a goddess. The name Everest was imposed on it by the British surveyors of the Great Trigonometrical Survey of India, who couldn't find a local name for it when they were mapping the Himalayas in the 19th century. It's named after Sir George Everest, who was once the Surveyor-General of India, though not at the time Everest was first discovered. It has to be one of the least appropriate names for any mountain anywhere. If they're going to name it after a person, they could at least name it after the one who discovered it, or the one who first climbed it, but no – instead it's named after some obscure Victorian geographer-cum-civil servant. In fact there *was* a local name for Everest, if anyone had bothered to ask the Sherpas. They know it as Chomolungma, the Mother Goddess and one of the five sisters of long life, ironic given the reputation Everest has now acquired for shortening lives.

Mark and I spend the morning trying to be IT technicians as we search for a solution which enables us to blog without the BGAN. Eventually we find one by transferring the files to Mark's Blackberry using the Micro SD card from my head camera, and

I'm able send out a blog post. For one reason or another too boring to explain in an adventure-travel diary we need to use a different method for updating my Tumblr blog. This involves Mark sending an email from his Blackberry to my iPhone, and I post it from there. After beavering away for most of the morning I'm finally able to update both sites, though it's going to be a bit of a hassle to do this on a regular basis.

The Altitude Junkies' base camp beneath Everest's North Face

The setting up of camp continues. They take the generator over to the Chinese camp, where a mechanic is able to get it working by replacing a part. The showers are now working too, and I have my first proper wash since leaving Kathmandu a week ago. The Sherpas start building a platform for our puja in a couple of days' time. With all this work to set up our luxury campsite it's easy to forget where we are. But for the plume on the summit, Everest remains clear all day; and at around 6.30, just before sunset, the whole of its North Face becomes bathed in a tangerine glow of sunlight. It really is a beautiful mountain from this side, and its features are becoming etched on our minds the longer we remain here. The North-East Ridge, Norton Couloir and summit pyramid crown the black North Face scoured by snow. 7,543m Changtse rises in front of the North Ridge and looks no more than a foothill.

I enjoyed the challenge of finding a solution for our base camp communications this morning, but I want to blog so it's something that interests me. The same can't be said of our cinema system. I don't really watch much telly when I'm at home, and I can't remember the last time I went to the cinema. In my opinion expeditions and cinema systems go together like guns and lunatics, and only end in pain and suffering. Perhaps I was traumatised by my experience at Base Camp on Cho Oyu a couple of years ago, when all anybody wanted to watch were violent action movies of no interest to me – yet I always seemed to be the poor sod squashed up against the far end of the dining tent with the cinema screen swinging across my dinner. When the rest of the team spend, quite literally, forty minutes talking about cables at dinner this evening it becomes too much for me. I have to go back to my tent and fetch ear plugs. There's only so long you can tolerate a conversation about VGA, HDMI, USB and iTunes on a mountain.

We christen the cinema by watching Ricky Gervais's *An Idiot Abroad*, a tongue-in-cheek documentary about a bigoted northerner travelling around China. Phil thinks it's funny because he says the main character, played by Karl Pilkington, looks and talks like me. He says I should try to become the first Karl Pilkington lookalike to climb Everest.

I'm happy to be the butt of Phil's jokes if it means we don't have to watch *The Bourne Insomnia*, or some other moronic action thriller. However, I'm not disappointed when the petrol generator chugs to a standstill in the cold of Base Camp and the lights go off.

DAY 7
REMEMBERING THE EVEREST DEAD

Tuesday, 17ᵗʰ of April 2012 – Base Camp, Everest, Tibet

It's another clear day at Base Camp, and in the morning I decide to do my first exercise of the expedition by taking a gentle stroll up to the Everest memorials on a small mound above the western side of camp. A bewildering number of stones have been erected in memory of those who have died trying to climb Everest, from the named and the unnamed, to the young and the old, the famous to the unknown. I guess that some of these people lost their lives trying to do something silly, like the French snowboarder Marco Siffredi, who died trying to snowboard down the Hornbein Couloir. Others probably found themselves fighting for their lives in marginal conditions. A small number may have been trying something beyond their abilities but carried on anyway because the mountain had become their obsession. I try to imagine that I'm too sensible to be any of these things, that I'm too cautious a mountaineer to lose my life up there, but you just don't know.

Somewhere at the back of camp is another memorial to the north side's best-known casualty, George Mallory. If anyone can be accused of having an obsession with getting to the top and dying because of it, then it's him. He famously said he wanted to climb Everest 'because it's there'. In 1924 he disappeared into the mist on the summit ridge with his climbing partner Sandy Irvine, never to be seen alive again. I wander slowly over to the memorial mound and bump into Margaret. Together we try to find the plaque to Mallory, but without success. The biggest memorial is wreathed in a tangle of prayer flags which hide any plaques there may be underneath. All the other memorials that we find in this area at the back of camp contain dedications in Chinese, so we give up and return to camp. I'll have to look for it again another time.

The Everest Base Camp memorials

Later in the morning Margaret gets a shock, and she decides to recount it to Mila (and the rest of us) at lunchtime as a warning.

'You need to be aware, Mila, that we're not the only people using the lady's shower. I tried to use it earlier today, but one of the Sherpas was in there.'

'Which one was it?' we ask.

'I don't know. I didn't see his face.'

We all roar with laughter.

'Did he have two legs or three?'

Grant spends the afternoon walking around Base Camp compiling an audit of everyone climbing Everest from the north this year. There are fifteen teams, comprising 109 'western' climbers including guides and leaders (a slightly misleading term, since some of the climbers classified as 'western' are Chinese or Japanese), and ninety-six climbing Sherpas. This is far more than I expected. It seems very quiet here at Base Camp, much more so than when I was here five years ago. This is probably because of the much higher cost of climbing permits now. Base Camp on the north side is spread out over a huge area, so it seems there are many more people here than it looks. I ask Phil if there are more than he expected.

'Dude, there were nearly that number of summits last year,' he replies.

This is his way of saying it's pretty quiet this year.

I'm settling nicely into the easy pace of life on an expedition in a remote part of the world, but this time I seem to be spending an inordinate amount of time stressing about technology. This afternoon I try to send a blog post about the base camp memorials, but Google Mail keeps refusing to send my messages because it thinks they're spam. After several attempts it even locks my account so I can no longer log in. I'm mystified and not happy. There is no reference in my emails to cheap Viagra or penis enlargement, so why block them? Luckily Mark, whose Blackberry I use to send the post, is very patient. We eventually get it posted by sending it from his own email address.

The theme of failing technology continues into the evening when we make another attempt to watch *An Idiot Abroad*. We've moved the cinema from the dome tent into one of the big yellow rectangular storage tents where there's more space. I begin by sitting at the back, where the sound of the generator is much louder than the film. I move forward, and we watch about twenty minutes before the generator dies again and everything goes dark. It's sad that even here among this beautiful landscape our lives seem to be dictated by the vagaries of modern technology. Still, at least we've now managed to watch a full episode, albeit in two separate sittings.

DAY 8
THE PUJA TO END ALL PUJAS

Wednesday, 18th of April 2012 – Base Camp, Everest, Tibet

It's the day of our puja today, the ceremony where we ask the mountain gods for safe passage. Monks from the Rongbuk Monastery have already arrived by the time I get up for breakfast at eight o'clock. They have decided it's too windy to conduct the ceremony outside, and have set up their altar in the Sherpa dining tent. Dorje is keen to get started, and even before we've finished eating we're ushered away from the breakfast table to unpack our ice axes, crampons and harnesses, and place them on the altar to be blessed.

The puja begins in sedate enough fashion, with the three monks chanting to appease the mountain deities. We gather round and watch with our heads bowed. It gets more entertaining when one of them notices a shoulder of meat hanging up in the corner. They consider this inauspicious, and to avoid jeopardising the rest of their prayers they tell Dorje they have to bless the carcass. Ang Gelu, wearing a red 1980s shell suit, is called upon to raise the meat and swing a large carving knife around while they continue chanting. The monks are young and amiable, and smile benignly as we chuckle at Ang Gelu's performance.

After an hour or two of chanting we go outside to raise the prayer flags. The Sherpas extend them like spokes of a wheel from a large flagpole on the puja platform they built a couple of days ago. They burn juniper twigs in a small furnace in the side of the platform, and we have to throw tsampa (flour) three times into the air to be taken by the wind. This part of the ceremony gets a bit messy, and Phil warned us beforehand to put on dirty clothes. After chucking their three handfuls, some people keep behind a bit extra to lob over each other. Protocol dictates that we smear a white paste over our noses and cheeks in the manner of the 1980s pop icon Adam Ant. The monks participate in this flour fight as enthusiastically as the Sherpas.

We return to the puja tent to complete the blessing, but after the monks depart the event turns into an all-day drinking session. Tuborg beers are cracked open and a pot of rakshi (home-made Nepali firewater) is passed around. The rakshi is lethal and tastes awful. With some sleight of hand I manage to finish my glass without any of the contents finding their way into my mouth. Nobody notices, and I refill the glass with beer. Mark, Ian and Grant, however, are made to drink several glasses.

After the rakshi Mark decides to teach us a drinking game which involves lifting a glass of beer off the floor with our teeth while doing the splits. Everyone takes part, with varying degrees of success and a few abject failures that are particularly entertaining. Pasang Ongchu proves to be the star man, and is flexible enough to complete the task without falling over; but he is soon upstaged by Grant, who has a party trick that involves drinking a whole glass of Tuborg while standing on his head.

Mark is particularly impressed.

'Quality, quality,' he cries as Grant drains the glass while holding it between his teeth.

Like Grant, Mark was once a rugby player, and post-match activities like these will once have formed an important part of his social calendar.

During a more introspective section of the afternoon we sit around in a big circle and take it in turns to criticise Ian for giving his oxygen away on Manaslu. By the time dinner is served at six o'clock, Mark and Grant have long since flopped out in their tents. Ian makes it to dinner, but finds conversation challenging.

We all have an early night. Now the puja has been completed we can at last start climbing the mountain.

DAY 9
AN AUSTRALIAN CLIMBING LEGEND

Thursday, 19th of April 2012 – Base Camp, Everest, Tibet

Phil turns up for breakfast this morning with a booming car stereo system and plonks it on the table. He looks at me, Mark and Ian.

'You bought this off a Tibetan during the puja yesterday. I wondered if you remember buying it?'

At some point after the chanting had finished and the drinking was in full swing, the Sherpas had a whip round for a stereo that a Tibetan on a motorbike was looking to sell. The price was 180 yuan. As this is only about thirty dollars, Mark, Ian and I decided to buy it for them. We're not sure what Phil thinks we're going to do with it, but we ask him to return it to them.

It's very calm this morning, another beautiful day with very light winds. They are blowing towards the mountain rather than away from it, as they have done until today. Phil tells us these are known as the *China winds*, which cancel out the prevailing weather and lead to calmer conditions. When the China winds blow later in the season it usually means a good summit window. It's certainly calm down here today, but the plume on Everest's summit grows as the morning passes. There have been very high winds up there all the time we've been here, often reaching as far down the mountain as the North Col.

We've been patient here at Base Camp. We've not been itching to move up the mountain, knowing that we have plenty of time and still need to acclimatise. But today we see the first signs of movement in the team. At lunchtime Phil announces we have forty yaks arriving tomorrow to carry our kit up to Advanced Base Camp (ABC). The Sherpas will go with them, and we'll follow the next day. I'll be excited to get moving at last.

In the afternoon we have a visit from the legendary Australian climber Andrew Lock, who completed all the 8,000m peaks in 2009 and is here this year because Everest is the only remaining 8,000er he hasn't climbed without supplementary oxygen. He's climbing independently, without Sherpa support, but is using Jamie McGuinness's base camp services. Jamie is an expedition leader from New Zealand who used to be Phil's business partner, and most of us know him. Phil seems to think that if Andrew reaches the summit he will do a full traverse into Nepal, using the tents provided by Jamie's team on the south side of Everest for his descent. This would probably mean he won't be allowed back into Tibet again, but Phil thinks he'll retire if he makes it up Everest this year, so he won't care if he's banned from Tibet.

Both Phil and Andrew drop hints about writing books. Although they have many stories to tell about climbing the 8,000m peaks, both are unusual because they seem to be waiting till the end of their careers before they do so. Jamie 'happens' to turn up at our dining tent on the dot of four o'clock, our usual time for happy hour, when we meet up for red wine, cheese and Pringles. Word seems to be getting around camp that we have a ready supply of alcohol, and it probably won't be the last time we see them at our dinner table.

DAY 10
REMEMBERING GEORGE MALLORY AND
SANDY IRVINE

Friday 20th of April, 2012 – Base Camp, Everest, Tibet

I'm up before breakfast this morning to finish packing my stuff
to go on the yaks up to Advanced Base Camp (ABC). Forty-eight
yaks arrive after breakfast to carry 1,800kg of equipment up
there. Seven of our Sherpas will go with them, and we follow
tomorrow. It's another beautiful, hot morning here at Base Camp,
and during the early part of it Chomolungma even lacks her
plume for the first time since we've been here.

Another climber watches the yak herders pack our
equipment, and Phil points him out as an Italian who travels
light, sleeps in other people's tents, and has a reputation for
stealing oxygen. I don't know whether he is being harsh or not.
Since permit fees have gone up here on the north side, most of
the shoestring maverick climbers have moved over to the south,
but if what Phil says is true and there's one of them here, it's a
real nuisance. Our Sherpas will be stocking our higher camps
with fuel, food and oxygen, ready for when we arrive there, and
if any of it is missing, particularly the oxygen, then it could
prove quite dangerous – our lives may depend on it. Strangely
the man comes over to our camp to ask if he can buy some of the
oxygen. The answer is no, of course – we've brought it for our
own use and not to sell to other people – but if he's prepared to
pay for it then why on earth hasn't he brought any of his own?

Dorje is very angry. It's his team who will be carrying each of the four-kilogram cylinders up the mountain to stock our camps. He points the Italian climber out to the other Sherpas, and in the afternoon he invites the Sherpas working with him over for rakshi. He tells them he will hold them responsible if any of our oxygen goes missing. The Sherpa community is very close-knit. Many of the people working on big mountains are related, and Dorje is highly respected. Hopefully this Italian climber won't cause any trouble for other teams.

In the afternoon I go to look for the Mallory memorial which I was unable to find a few days ago. A funny incident happened after I blogged about my failure to locate it. Someone from Dubai commented on my blog post and provided a link to Grant's website, saying there was a useful map of Base Camp on it. He was unaware that I could simply walk over to Grant's tent and ask him. Grant's 'map' is actually a panoramic photo of the whole of camp taken from one of the hillsides above us. He's added labels to the photo showing the locations of the various teams, and I imagine if I was following the Everest season from home then I would find it quite interesting. It isn't much help to me now, though, as it only shows general locations, and I'm looking for a precise one. My problem the other day was finding Mallory's memorial among the dozens of other ones. Today I am successful. Although it's not the biggest, the plaque is quite shiny and substantial and I was a bit of an idiot not to notice it before.

Of all the people who have died here on the north side of Everest, George Mallory made the most significant contribution to future climbs. In three expeditions, in 1921, 1922 and 1924, he discovered and pioneered the route up the East Rongbuk Glacier, North Col Wall and North-East Ridge that most people follow to climb Everest from Tibet. He was also a convert to the use of bottled oxygen, having been impressed by the performance of rival climber George Finch when he used it on the 1922 expedition. Mallory chose the youngster Sandy Irvine as his climbing partner in 1924 because he was good with the oxygen apparatus. The two were last seen alive climbing a prominent step on the summit ridge by teammate Noel Odell before the mist swept over and they were never seen again.

Mallory's body was found in 1999, and from the broken rope around his waist and the large hole in his cheekbone, it was evident that he had taken a fall. His sunglasses were in his pocket, suggesting that he was probably descending in the dark. Nobody knows whether Mallory and Irvine reached the summit, but in my opinion it doesn't matter. Mallory was a great climber whose name is synonymous with the history of Everest, but he didn't get back down. The bewildering array of memorials at Base Camp is a reminder that reaching the summit is only half the climb. For lesser climbers like me the summit would be great, but getting down is the important bit.

Our plan for the next few days is to walk up to ABC and spend a few nights there before climbing as high as 7,500m to acclimatise. If we are successful it will put us in position for an early summit push; we could return to Base Camp to await a weather window. But later this afternoon Phil gets a forecast suggesting there may be a storm in three days' time. If true, it will give us just enough time to tag the North Col, but means we will have to come down again and do a second rotation. I don't mind this; in many ways I'd prefer two shorter rotations to one long one. I don't like to rush things and will feel stronger if I can spend more time acclimatising.

In the evening Phil and Margaret reminisce about their 2010 Everest expedition. One of their climbers got into trouble on summit day. Phil was returning from the summit and reached the Balcony, a flattish area at about 8,400m on Everest's south side summit route. Here he found Dorje sitting vigil over an unconscious man, one of their clients. Dorje had given up hope for the man, but he wouldn't leave him. Phil managed to get him conscious again by injecting dexamethasone, but he became violent and refused to accept help. The rescue became a real struggle. The man threw several bottles of oxygen down the Lhotse Face, and Dorje had to keep hitting him to make him cooperate.

Back at their hotel in Kathmandu people were in tears because the rescue had been successful. He was still alive when he should have been dead, but the real tragedy was that he remained in denial about the help he received. He never thanked anyone, or even accepted that it happened, despite being presented with video evidence taken by some of the people who helped him.

I know I could never climb Everest without assistance, and whatever happens up there, I'm determined that I won't forget to acknowledge those who help me.

DAY 11
TO YAKSHIT CAMP

Saturday 21st of April, 2012 – Interim Camp, Everest, Tibet

We set off at ten o'clock this morning for our first foray up the mountain. It's our first cloudy day at Base Camp and there's a slight wind in the air. It's a day for fleeces.

I set off with Mark and Ian, but they shoot off ahead of me before we've even reached the terminal moraine at the front of Base Camp. Mark is pre-acclimatised after trekking to Everest Base Camp on the south side with his girlfriend Claire before the expedition, and Ian is a boy racer. It takes me two hours to walk up the left-hand side of the Rongbuk Glacier to the point where the East Rongbuk Glacier, our route of ascent, branches to the left. It's sunny and dusty, and the route is mainly on the flat, but beyond the junction the East Rongbuk rises steeply and the climb becomes very tiring. Everest is visible all the way up the Rongbuk Glacier, though it's mostly in cloud, but when I turn up the East Rongbuk it soon disappears behind a wall of crumbly brown rock that comes down from Changtse.

Grant and Margaret overtake me. As they walk past, Grant pauses, turns to me and says, 'Margaret just told me her training schedule.'

'What's that, then?'

'She gets up at five o'clock in the morning and cycles to work. She gets there at six o'clock and goes to the gym for an hour, and then she goes and does her work for about nine hours. Then at the end of the day she cycles home, so it's a round trip of about fifty kilometres of cycling. Then she gets home, has a small rest for about twenty minutes and then gets on the treadmill.'

Margaret has been throwing rocks at Grant, but neither of us have noticed, so engrossed are we in the conversation. I look at her and see that she's only carrying a very small pack today.

'Margaret, will you carry my pack for me, please?' I ask her.

But Grant hasn't finished yet. 'And then at the weekend she does two hundred kilometres of cycling as well. So I said to her, "How many days per week do you train like this?", and she said, "Oh, just seven".'

They continue onwards, and I'm left to consider that I'm almost certainly going to get beaten up the mountain by a 62-year-old lady. There was a time in the past when this would have shamed me beyond words, but now I'm not so sure.

Trekking in the main Rongbuk Valley, with Everest up ahead

I continue plodding slowly, unconcerned by the pace. I reach Japanese Base Camp, a flattish area where the high-walled valley widens, and I remember it from when I camped here with Mark and Ian in 2007. I'm making good time and I find a comfortable rock to sit on while I stop for a packed lunch. In the afternoon the weather changes, and I complete the rest of the rocky ascent to Interim Camp in light snowfall, with a cold wind at my back. My thin liner gloves are not warm enough; I have to put my trekking pole away so that I can walk with my hands in my pockets. Mist descends and visibility is reduced, but lots of people are walking up today, and there are always figures ahead of me to show me the way.

I reach Interim Camp at 3.15. I'm happy that my Achilles tendon has held up pretty well. It's been troubling me for the last three months and has limited the amount of training I've been able to do for Everest. I was still feeling the injury when I came out to Nepal, but perhaps the week of doing nothing at Base Camp was just what my tendon needed. Total rest wasn't possible while I was still working, and now I just need to hope the many years of preparation for this adventure will compensate for my lack of physical training.

Interim Camp isn't the most comfortable place I've ever stayed. There are lots of pointy rocks underneath my tent, and we've christened it Yakshit Camp – Phil said it's one of the dirtiest places he's ever camped in, with so much yak shit lying about that it floats around in the air and gets into your lungs. Someone always ends up getting ill here, he told us, but I presume the aerial yak shit only appears when it's hot and dusty. With the damp mist and snow we've had today the air is much cleaner.

I find myself sharing a tent with Grant, and he turns out to be a good tent mate, with one reservation: he's a talker. Tired after the big jump in altitude today, I'd prefer to spend the afternoon snoozing, but instead we talk non-stop for the next two hours. It's not that Grant is boring; it's just relentless.

He tells me about the time he got high-altitude pulmonary edema (HAPE) at Advanced Base Camp last year.

'We were going to climb up to the North Col, but I didn't get very far before I felt like shit and had to come back down again.

Then I woke up coughing blood in the middle of the night. I could hear my lungs gurgling – the classic symptoms of HAPE. I had to get out of my tent to go and be sick, but I could only crawl about five metres. I had no energy.'

'Did Jamie hear you and get up to help?' I ask. (Jamie McGuinness was Grant's expedition leader last year.)

'Everybody was up sleeping at the North Col. There was just me and one Tibetan kitchen boy down at ABC. I had to lie awake for the next five hours until I could make a radio call up to the North Col at 6.30. Jamie told me what drugs to take and instructed me to descend immediately. Going back down to Base Camp was hell. I had no energy and there were times when I had to crawl.'

Remarkably, he recovered sufficiently to make a summit attempt a few weeks later. He seems to be acclimatising much better this year.

DAY 12
THE MAGIC HIGHWAY

Sunday 22nd of April, 2012 – Advanced Base Camp (ABC),
Everest, Tibet

We're woken up with breakfast at the tent door at around six o'clock. I can't face the noodle soup Pemba brings at this hour of the morning, but I accept a bread roll. Grant, on the other hand, eats not only his own noodle soup but mine as well, and continues to talk for New Zealand. By 6.30 he has already asked me whether I have any plans to write a book, whether I'm interested in travelling to the polar regions, and if I ever write technical blog posts. All of these questions require considered responses. My brain isn't capable of processing the answers at this time of the morning, and to make matters worse the bread roll is demanding all my attention. I chew and chew and chew some more, but nothing seems to happen. It takes me half an hour to finish the job, and much of the bread sticks to my teeth to be digested in my body's own time.

Grant and I leave Interim Camp at 7.30 for what is going to prove a tough day. Immediately out of camp the trail drops fifty metres to cross a cleft in the ice, then rises steeply again to join the Magic Highway, a strip of medial moraine up the middle of the East Rongbuk Glacier. This remarkable natural highway provides a non-technical trail up to Advanced Base Camp which even yaks can follow. It's a tough climb and I tire very quickly, but up ahead is a closer view of Everest and the North-East

Ridge, our first since yesterday morning. The glacier all around is riven by dramatic ice pinnacles which we christened *sharks' fins* last time we were here. The glacier would be extremely difficult, if not impossible, to navigate without the solid surface of the Magic Highway.

Everest and shark's fin from the Magic Highway

It's not easy terrain underfoot. At the top of the hill we have to stop to let some yaks past, belonging to the large Russian 7 Summits Club team. Grant shoots off ahead of me, and from now on it's going to be a slow plod with a heavy pack resting on my shoulders, containing the sleeping bag and mat I needed at Interim Camp. As I slowly place one foot in front of the other, I calculate that I have 600m of ascent today, which means I can expect to have six hours of it. Although it's bright and sunny, a bitter wind whips up, and I stop to put on a windproof layer.

After three hours of walking the trail descends off the moraine to Changtse Base Camp, where we camped five years ago after our second day up the East Rongbuk Valley. I'm now directly beneath the northern flanks of Changtse, the smaller 7,583m peak which lies between Everest and Base Camp. Everest itself is out of view again, behind the lower peak.

It's a spectacular area of ice lakes and ice pinnacles, but I'm exhausted and don't appreciate it like I might. I stop for a bite to eat while the wind blasts spindrift into my face. It isn't pleasant and I stand up to continue. Immediately a gust takes the green rubber sit-mat I was resting on into the air, tumbling it hundreds of yards over a snow mound. There's no chance of recovering it, and in a few short minutes it will probably be miles away.

It's 10.30 and I've completed only a third of today's ascent. I steel myself for another four hours of slow plod, shoulder my pack and continue. About fifteen minutes out of Changtse Base Camp I catch up with Grant and Margaret taking a rest, and we complete most of the onward ascent together. There are some interesting ice formations to negotiate to get back onto the moraine, but once back on the Magic Highway it's a monotonous trudge. As we round the eastern edge of Changtse, Everest appears again. Its black face now looks too daunting to contemplate. The bitterly cold gusts of wind begin to take their toll, and I can feel my fingers getting cold in the inadequate liner gloves – all I've brought with me for this two-day hike. I pack my trekking pole away and walk with my hands in my pockets again. This helps a little.

I'm glad when one of our Tibetan kitchen boys appears over a ridge of moraine about half an hour out of camp, carrying a flask of hot lemon. I stop for a few minutes to warm my fingers on the hot metal cup, and I find this as pleasing as the drink itself.

Seeing the tents of ABC up ahead is a morale boost. We have to wait for more yaks to pass, but otherwise I'm able to continue without a break and arrive at 1.30. The Sherpas have pitched our tents at the top end of camp, so we have further to walk, but I don't mind. Phil is there to welcome us, and Pasang Ongchu brings my big red North Face duffle bag, which the yaks carried up here yesterday, over to my tent. It's been an exhausting day, but I'm unconcerned. We've made a very quick jump to 6,410m – an extreme altitude, carrying big packs. Phil tells me even some of the Sherpas are feeling tired, although this is probably just to cheer me up. They arrived a day earlier and have been busy setting up camp.

It's great to be ushered into a cosy Mountain Hardwear dome tent as soon as I arrive, with table and chairs, hot drinks and biscuits. We try to force some lunch down, but it's going to be difficult to eat here until we're properly acclimatised. Although ABC is in a beautiful location, I have days here to admire the scenery and don't take it all in now.

It's not very pleasant outside while the icy gusts continue – much warmer inside the tent with the sun on it. It's an afternoon for snoozing indoors and getting some energy back, though my tent takes one hell of a buffeting. Sleep isn't easy.

DAY 13
EVEREST LASSITUDE

Monday 23ʳᵈ of April, 2012 – Advanced Base Camp (ABC),
Everest, Tibet

In *The Ascent of Rum Doodle* by W.E. Bowman, they called it base camp lassitude, the desire to be in your sleeping bag and do nothing all day. There's a lot of it about right now. Everything takes so much effort up here, from climbing out of your tent to visit the toilet, to sorting out kit, to walking the few short feet to the dining tent for hot drinks; the smallest of tasks leaves you out of breath. It hasn't been helped by the wind, which has remained gusty all morning. It's not very tempting to get out of your tent when it's bending at forty-five degrees.

Fortunately we don't have to do anything for a few days. Phil's weather forecast says it's going to remain windy until the 26th, which would give us three days to rest and acclimatise in ABC. Certainly I don't feel like going up to the North Col in the gusty winds we've had this morning. If it's calmer tomorrow I may go out for a wander around camp, but for now I'm content to rest.

DAY 14
THE VIEW FROM ABC

Tuesday 24ᵗʰ of April, 2012 – Advanced Base Camp (ABC),
Everest, Tibet

When I experience broken sleep – waking up incessantly throughout the night with a banging headache, rolling over and trying to go back to sleep again – it's difficult to imagine that I'm becoming acclimatised, but hopefully I am. After two days here at ABC I still have very little appetite. It seems to need six times as many chews as it does at sea level to force down a tiny plate of food. In the evening it's worse. At six o'clock the temperature is so low that my food can't stay warm for longer than a couple of minutes, and I end up eating most of it cold.

I'm not alone. Everybody is suffering, and I can't expect to climb this mountain without enduring hardship. Margaret has twice been on the south side of Everest, and summited last year. She looks as rough as anyone at breakfast this morning, even Mark (well, OK, maybe not Mark). She says that it's harder here on the north side, with two big leaps to high altitude – first to Base Camp at 5,160m where we spent a week, and now here to ABC at 6,410m, where we intend to spend a week more. There's none of the gradual gain in altitude that you get trekking into Base Camp on the south side, or any of the *climb high, sleep low* style of acclimatisation which triggers the body to generate red blood cells, helping you to acclimatise more quickly. Although I can't imagine having the energy to climb up to the North Col, I expect it will do me the power of good when we eventually get round to it. We still have high winds forecast for the next couple of days, so the plan is to go up to the North Col on Thursday if everyone is feeling up to it.

Tent lassitude prevails this morning, compounded by the bitterly cold wind that continues to gust from time to time. From my tent I keep hearing people getting up to go outside, and uttering various colourful and creative expletives. There's not much variation, but it persuades me to stay indoors for much of the morning.

I do manage to get some jobs done inside my tent. I practice with all the straps, pockets and zips on my new Mountain Hardwear down suit, and discover that it has a *shit hole* down the back and sides, which enables me to unzip and take my trousers down while I'm still wearing it. With practice this is likely to come in very handy. There are stories of mountaineers having to pull the entire suit down around their ankles in order to take a crap, only to shit in the hood and not realise until they put it back over their head. I can imagine few things more unpleasant than this. On balance I would prefer to stick my arm down the suit and crap into my cupped hand.

After the marvellous discovery of my shit hole – a sentence I would never have predicted myself saying – I experiment with various glove and camera combinations I expect to be using at different stages of the climb, to ensure I'll be able to operate the cameras effectively. What I don't know yet, and won't know till I get up there, is how the gloves and cameras will cope with the cold.

Just before lunch I go for an hour's wander around camp, my first since arriving here. I walk down to the bottom of camp and watch some ice climbers practising with ropes and ice tools on the edge of the East Rongbuk Glacier. This brings back some memories – it's what Mark, Ian and I did when we came here five years ago, much less experienced climbers than we are now. At the time I had never abseiled properly or used fixed ropes and a jumar before, and I needed the skills for our ascent of Lhakpa Ri and climb up to the North Col. Lhakpa Ri is a gentle mountain that rises up to 7,045m across the East Rongbuk Glacier to our east. At least it seemed quite gentle five years ago. It was just an easy snow slog, although we climbed it in a blizzard which made things more tiring. This year it looks much harder, with a couple of steep ice sections.

Lhakpa Ri from Advanced Base Camp

To the left of Lhakpa Ri is a slightly rockier peak, Khartaphu, and left of this the glacier swings round behind the flanks of Changtse and disappears from sight. This is the route we came up a couple of days ago. To the right of Lhakpa Ri is a gentle snow col, the Rapui La, before Everest's ragged North-East Ridge rises sharply. The view of Everest from ABC is dominated by a feature on the North-East Ridge known as The Pinnacles, a jagged knife edge where the legendary British climbers Pete Boardman and Joe Tasker met their end in 1982. The summit itself peeps up inconspicuously to the right of The Pinnacles.

We'll be taking an easier route up to the North-East Ridge which thankfully avoids The Pinnacles altogether. This involves climbing a steep section of ice, the North Col Wall, some distance above camp at the top end of the East Rongbuk Glacier. This wall leads up to the North Col, the saddle between Everest and Changtse. It looks daunting and quite sheer from here, but I know from experience that it isn't. Changtse towers directly over ABC in a wall of rock. It cuts off the sun abruptly at 3.30 in the afternoon, making it instantly very cold. I wonder what it will be like climbing up to the North Col the day after tomorrow. Other peaks that I've ascended again, such as Mera Peak and Aconcagua, have been much easier the second time around because I was much more experienced. I hope it will be the same here.

Pemba serves a delicious meal of fried yak and chips for lunch. Although I still eat very slowly I can feel a little bit of my appetite returning. It's bliss lying in my tent and snoozing with the sun on it for a couple of hours after lunch. The hardship begins when the sun dips behind Changtse in the middle of the afternoon, and I know it will continue until it rises again tomorrow morning. Pemba produces yak steak and roast potatoes for dinner, which is very tasty but exceedingly tough. In fact, it's so tough that I wonder if I expend more energy sawing it into pieces than I gain from eating it. My teeth take a pummelling. After what seems an age I eventually finish it, and take consolation in the fact that my appetite seems to be improving.

DAY 15
A WALK TO CRAMPON POINT

Wednesday 25th of April, 2012 – Advanced Base Camp (ABC),
Everest, Tibet

Some of the early forays up to the North Col are made today.
Our Sherpa team leaves at 7.30 this morning to deposit a cache of
equipment up there, and we intend to follow them tomorrow to
tag the col and gain some altitude.

Every night here at ABC I seem to sleep a little longer and
wake with a little less of a headache, but I don't think the latter
will vanish completely until I've climbed higher. After breakfast I
decide to go for a short walk up to Crampon Point, where the
moraine ends and the glacier begins. It's so named because it's
the place where you need to put on crampons if you want to
climb any higher. It takes me about an hour to get there, but it's
good exercise up a trail of moraine and over patches of ice which
are relatively easy to cross in just my approach shoes. (I don't
mean *just* my approach shoes, of course. I had the rest of my
clothes on too, but I wasn't wearing my heavy mountaineering
boots.)

I walk very slowly, almost as slowly as I've been eating,
although at least when I walk there is evidence of progress at
every step, which hasn't always been the case with chewing. I
reach Crampon Point at 11.30, and according to my altimeter I've
ascended 150m from ABC, which is good headway.

Above me is a plateau of ice, and where it ends the North Col

Wall rises up to Camp 1. This is the steepest, most technical section of the whole ascent, and it looks quite daunting; but Mark, Ian and I completed it as far as the North Col in 2007, and this gives me more confidence. It looks like quite a few people have chosen to climb it today, and I count around fifty figures on the Wall. Nearly half are bunched together on a steep bottleneck section through seracs just beneath the col. Although I can't see the very base of the climb from where I stand, this looks to be the hardest bit.

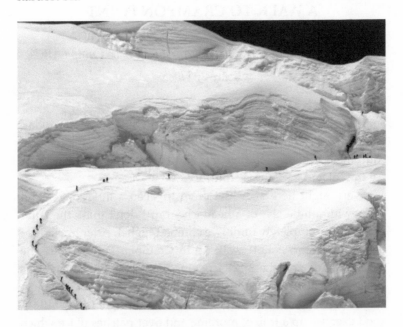

Climbers on the North Col Wall

Pleased with my little outing, I wander slowly back to camp. I need to take care crossing a couple of the icy sections in my shoes, but I get over them without a hitch and arrive back in camp at 12.30. It was an easy stroll completed very slowly, and it's raised my spirits a great deal. There's nothing worse for morale than cowering in your tent all day listening to the wind bash against it. It's been good to get out and about.

Unlike at Base Camp, up here at ABC Phil has managed to

get the BGAN connection working on his laptop, and at lunch he shows us the latest weather forecast. The jet stream is returning. Tomorrow is going to be pretty much our last chance to get up to the col for a while, and it may well be very windy up there. There's not much point in hanging around at ABC any longer after we've tagged the col, so the following day we'll head back to the comforts of Base Camp and await a suitable window for a second rotation. I'll be very happy to be down there again, as I've been finding it hard up here at ABC.

After a brief snooze I spend the afternoon slowly getting my kit together for tomorrow's climb. At dinner time in our cosy mess tent, Phil decides to play the clown. He asks whether we want packed lunches for the climb tomorrow. When I ask whether it's possible to have a chocolate bar instead of a hard-boiled egg – in my experience a regular but awkward ingredient of expedition packed lunches – he acts out an exuberant performance of somebody clipping and unclipping from a fixed rope as they pick away at the shell of their egg.

'Oops, I've dropped some shell. "Egg",' he cries at the top of his voice, mimicking what climbers shout to the next person on the rope when they dislodge a loose rock (obviously they shout 'rock' rather than 'egg').

It's nice to know some people still have bundles of energy at these extreme altitudes. Unfortunately for Phil he seems to be the only person who does, and while I'm sure his performance would have been hilarious at sea level, it meets with blank stares now. If we weren't too high for vegetation to grow, then I imagine tumbleweed would be blowing across the tent.

DAY 16
CLIMBING THE NORTH COL WALL

Thursday 26th of April, 2012 – Advanced Base Camp (ABC),
Everest, Tibet

We leave ABC shortly after eight o'clock and begin the slow plod
up to Crampon Point. I find myself walking with Mila and Dorje,
but I'm very weary as we start, and suffering from cold fingers.
What was easy yesterday, wearing my light approach shoes and
carrying just my camera, is a struggle this morning wearing my
huge *La Sportiva Olympus Mons* boots for the first time and
carrying all my climbing equipment in my pack.

I'm not even out of camp when I have to stop and massage
my fingers. Although they will probably warm up very slowly as
I climb, I don't want them painfully cold for the next hour, as
often happens in these situations. Mila waits patiently, but the
no-nonsense Dorje is keen to keep moving, so he makes me take
my heavy-duty down mitts out of my pack and put them on.
They are excessively large for this gentle morning walk, but they
do the job, and within ten minutes of putting them on my hands
are so warm I can feel the sweat dripping from my fingers.

We reach Crampon Point at 9.30, and it's taken me half an
hour longer than yesterday. Ian and Grant are ahead of us; Mark,
Margaret and Chedar catch us up as we put our crampons and
harnesses on. I lead slowly onto the ice, with Mila and Dorje
behind me. Although I feel like I have very little energy, I know
I'll keep pushing forward slowly for as long as I need to. Beyond

Crampon Point a broad plateau of ice leads the way up to the North Col Wall, and ahead of me figures trudge slowly across it.

The wall is impressive; it looks vertical, and I remember feeling intimidated as I approached it five years ago. I know that it's not so vertical though, and things will be fine as soon as I start climbing it. The cold wind that gusts across us and cuts through our bones is more of a concern this time. Mark overtakes, but then decides to turn around. It's very cold when the wind blasts, and he has his own fingers to worry about too. They are his Achilles heel. They are more than usually susceptible to frostbite and have prevented him from climbing peaks in the past, most notably on Manaslu last year. We all want to get as high as possible today, but we also want to return unscathed. This first rotation is not the time for doing anything silly. Mark makes a wise decision by returning to ABC.

Mila, Dorje and I rest briefly at the foot of the wall, but again Dorje is keen to keep moving. Another group of climbers arrived at the same time as us, and he wants to start up the ropes ahead of them. It's a good move: once we begin climbing we're quicker than they are, and Margaret and Chedar are only a little slower as they clip in behind us.

Ice conditions can change significantly from year to year. I soon discover the route up the wall is much steeper than it was when I climbed it five years ago. I remember two steep sections back then, at the very bottom and the very top, but in between the fixed ropes zigzagged at a gentler gradient. This time the bottom section is blue ice; it's rock hard and difficult to get a foothold. I inch up gingerly and find it tiring. Above it the trail zigzags more gently, but steep and exposed sections keep me alert. We make good progress and not everyone is finding it as tiring as I am. The rest of our Sherpa team comes skipping down the ropes above us, having carried loads up to the North Col for the second successive day.

They're not the only ones finding it easy.

'Can you smell burning?' Mila asks me when we stop for a short rest.

We turn round and see that Dorje has taken the opportunity

to light a cigarette. This becomes a problem for him when Mila and I decide to continue. He only has two hands, and he needs to choose between cigarette, jumar and ice axe.

He slides the axe into his harness and follows behind us.

Mila and Dorje traverse a section of the North Col Wall

Phil is as strong as a Sherpa, and shortly after midday he is the next to come racing down the ropes after tagging the North Col. He tells us we're not far from the top now, but he's concerned about the wind. He says if we get too cold then we should be happy with our day's work and turn back. At the next flattish section Mila decides to do just that, and she and Dorje head back down.

I manage to get my hands warmed up a little and am determined to continue, but the next section is very steep and exposed. When I see Margaret and Chedar turn around below me I begin to have second thoughts. While I don't mind walking on my own, for steep technical climbing like this I prefer the reassurance of a companion. Ian and Grant are still above me but there's no longer anyone behind. From studying the face yesterday, I know that there's a gentler traverse above this steep section, followed by an even steeper climb up onto the col. At my current rate of ascent I estimate there's probably still another hour of climbing before I reach it. I look at my altimeter and see that it's reading 6,900m. I decide to turn around. The climb will have done me some good, and there's no need to turn it into a lonely ordeal.

I'm a confident enough ascender, but I'm not so fearless going down when I'm staring at the exposed slopes below me. I descend with great care, watching Margaret and Chedar become ants in the distance as they climb down much more quickly. I need three abseils to get down the blue ice section at the foot of the wall. As I'm waiting at the bottom taking a drink, I see Ian come skipping down, confidently arm-wrapping Sherpa-style. These slopes are no problem for him; he's been all the way up to the col and back down again, and still he's caught me up. What a guy. He's definitely the star performer in our team (not including Sherpas and Phil, of course).

My return to ABC is a slow trudge. The winds are howling across the ice plateau, and I feel like I could be towing a sledge across Antarctica. I stumble back into camp at 2.30, satisfied though a little disappointed I didn't make it to the col. Grant is the only other member of our team to climb all the way up there; he arrives back in camp at four o'clock. Tomorrow we'll be descending to the comforts of Base Camp, and I spend the remainder of the day forcing down what food I can and snoozing.

DAY 17
THE SWEETEST BEER IN THE WORLD

Friday 27th of April, 2012 – Base Camp, Everest, Tibet

The plan is to have breakfast at the usual time of eight o'clock, then pack our kit bags in a leisurely fashion and descend to Base Camp. That's the theory, but I know from experience how keen Sherpas usually are to get moving. I decide to begin packing before breakfast, at seven o'clock. Despite the early hour, I expect at any minute to hear the telltale *click-click* of my tent being taken down around me. Most of us have the same thought, and we're nearly all ready to leave straight after breakfast.

As far as picturesque campsites go, Advanced Base Camp is up there among the finest in the world, but we're not sorry to be leaving. It's one of the harshest places to live that I will ever experience. I've been plagued by headaches for days. I have picked at my food despite Pemba producing some excellent meals, and the thin air has made the smallest of tasks exhausting. The crashing of the wind has been a constant companion. I know I will probably have to spend another couple of weeks up here if I'm to climb this mountain, but at least I'm prepared for it. I'm keeping my fingers crossed my body remains strong enough and my mind isn't too dulled.

For some reason the girl racer Mila again decides my lumbering pace is just the thing for getting back down to Base Camp, and we leave together at 8.30. Ian and Mark start out just a little ahead of us, but Ian seems to be more tired today, perhaps because of his greater exertions yesterday, and isn't rushing at his usual pace. We catch up with them quite quickly when we see Mark's pack by the side of the trail with no sign of its owner. Presumably the Sherpas were a bit too eager taking the toilet tent down this morning before Mark had a chance to use it.

The monotonous descent to Base Camp takes five and a half hours. Several sections seem to take for ever, and there are some parts I don't recognise from our ascent. There is less snow for sure. The Changtse Base Camp area was carpeted in white when we came through, and now it's just stones and rubble. Yakshit Camp lives up to its name without the snow. I stop to photograph an area which looks more like a farmer's paddock than a glacier camp.

Below this the land is dry and dusty. The dust gets into my lungs, and the wind is painful against my cheeks. It feels like a cold desert region. Only when we reach Japanese Base Camp, with the main Rongbuk Valley visible beneath us, do I gain heart. Mark and Ian have been ahead for a while, but I put on a burst of speed to catch up with them. My pace doesn't seem to matter for Mila; she is always right behind me. Had she decided to descend with Phil or the Sherpas then I expect she would have been able to keep up.

The four of us reach Base Camp a little before two o'clock, and Phil is standing outside to welcome us with some tins of Red Bull. While this might work for Mila the teetotaller, he takes some convincing that what the rest of us need most is Tuborg beer.

I dump all my kit in the porch of my tent and return to the dining tent. It's spotlessly clean. The carpet seems to have been vacuumed; Da Pasang can't have had much to do while we were up at ABC. It feels like a palace after our sufferings above, and for the first hour the sun shines in and it's cosy and warm. As for the Tuborg, I think it's the sweetest beer I've ever tasted, and when I tell the others they all agree.

Grant and Margaret arrive an hour later in a howling blizzard, but the rest of the day is very pleasant as we relax from our exertions. After a couple of beers Ian vanishes to the kitchen tent and reappears with a tray of wine. He repeats this trick several times, and nobody tries to stop him. In the tent next door we can hear Sherpa music and laughter – it's clear they're spending their afternoon in the same way as we are. The main disappointment for me is when Da Pasang produces the most beautiful roast chicken for dinner and I discover my appetite still hasn't returned. Mark, as is his habit, has the brilliant idea of introducing some drinking games. By 7.30 it's dark outside, but nobody can be bothered to get up and switch the lights on, so we sit around the table and continue talking in pitch blackness.

When I retire to my tent I spend several minutes groping through my backpack trying to find my head torch. It's only after I've bashed my head several times on the portable light above my head – thoughtfully provided by Phil for all our tents – that I realise I can just reach up and switch it on.

DAY 18
EVEREST NEWS

Saturday 28th of April, 2012 – Base Camp, Everest, Tibet

Throughout the night I listen to the sound of the wind buffeting my tent. Even though I'm wearing ear plugs it's still extremely loud, and it continues for all of the following day. I can't remember the last time I didn't have to listen to it: probably when I was back in Kathmandu nearly three weeks ago.

I'm feeling very tired today and can't summon up the energy to do very much, but it's nice to have a shower and a shave after several days. It takes me longer than usual to write my diary. I know I should blog, but my brain isn't really working yet, and it can wait till tomorrow.

We spend time today catching up on news from other Everest teams, mainly by reading Alan Arnette's Everest website and *Everest1953.co.uk*. I use my Kindle for internet access. It's not the most reliable means of web browsing, and it often takes several minutes to open a page, but it's the cheapest, and we have all day to wait.

We learn that two Sherpas have died, and there have been a couple of major avalanches and an electrical storm, all on the south side of the mountain. By contrast, here on the north all is quiet and everything is going to plan – so far. Alan Arnette has called it the 'dark side' of the mountain because of the lack of information he's been able to glean from expedition blogs. But 'dark side' makes it sounds like there are people wandering around camp dressed as Darth Vader.

We also try to get news from the outside world. This comes from Mark's daily update by satellite phone which his girlfriend Claire provides. It mostly consists of English Premier League and European Champions League football results. We try to convince Phil there's been a terrorist attack on Woodstock, the small town where he lives in New York State.

'Yeah, kidnapping Charlie Brown's canary is about as low as you can get.'

'Apparently Snoopy is distraught and has stolen Linus's security blanket.'

But either Phil has never read the *Peanuts* cartoon or he has other things on his mind today, because he doesn't seem to find us funny.

Meanwhile Ian's craving for alcohol seems to be reaching breaking point. Phil has imposed a three-unit limit during happy hour, which Ian reaches within minutes. He has started racking up a tab, which involves drinking a couple of units more and going into 'alcohol debt'. It's not clear how this is going to be repaid at the end of the expedition, but he is keeping us entertained. He sits at the table in excited anticipation, waiting for permission to go to the kitchen and get the next round.

'So, Ian, are you looking forward to your next drink?' Grant asks at one point, like someone asking a small child whether they're looking forward to a ride on the dodgems. It produces a few hearty chuckles around the table. Luckily Ian doesn't seem to mind being the butt of our jokes.

DAY 19
HOW COLD THE WIND DOTH BLOW

Sunday 29ᵗʰ of April , 2012 – Base Camp, Everest, Tibet

There's an eerie calm when I wake up this morning, and I realise the wind isn't pounding the life out of my tent for the first time in heaven knows how long. It doesn't last, though. Within an hour of breakfast the maddening sound of the flapping of tent nylon begins again, and continues all day. It's noisy and relentless. I'm finding it increasingly hard to remember the sound of silence.

I spend an exciting morning washing clothes. We've converted one of the storage tents into a laundry tent, where washing lines are hung and clothes put out to dry. With the wind as it is, hanging the washing line across your own tent in the traditional manner would mean that, within minutes, clothes would be covered with a fine silver powder and dirtier than when they started – fine if you like sequined outfits, but that's not really my style.

At lunch we spend some time discussing the latest weather forecast, which suggests there may be a lull in the wind on the 4th, 5th and 6th (which at the present moment seems about as likely as a team of yetis arriving in camp and starting up a barbecue). Phil says that if there's an early summit window – for example, the 10th – then we need to be prepared to stay up at ABC, rest for a few days, then go for it. But from my previous experience of very high altitude, I'm fairly sure that not only will

I need a second rotation up to the North Col to further acclimatise, but I will need to be well rested back at Base Camp again before I embark on a summit push. ABC is not a place to rest – unless my appetite improves dramatically on the second rotation then I'm going to continue wasting away up there.

It's an afternoon for blogging now that our high-altitude brains are slowly beginning to return. Grant writes an epic post which covers the whole of the first rotation in great detail, and the hardships he experienced at every moment (which happily doesn't include talking to his boring old tent mate at Interim Camp). It's a great record of life at high altitude, but may lead anyone reading it to wonder why on earth we bother.

My blog post is a more concise and frivolous one, which mentions the hardships in a few short sentences and probably leaves the impression life up there isn't so bad after all. Both of us write headlines that emphasise the wind as the enduring factor in our lives. It's so loud and annoying today that Phil decides to begin happy hour fifteen minutes early, at 3.45.

Ian leads the charge again, and five hours later he, Mark, Phil and I are still sitting in the same chairs in the dining tent, having a heated debate about whether China will be the next superpower. Snatches of this conversation would probably land some of us in prison if the Communist authorities could hear it. We haven't moved from our chairs all evening, other than to run back to our tents for warmer clothes when the sun vanished behind the hills at five o'clock.

DAY 20
EVEREST BLOG WARS

Monday 30th of April, 2012 – Base Camp, Everest, Tibet

It's generally agreed that today is the worst the wind has been so far. The sky is clear, and to begin with Chomolungma doesn't even wear her plume of cloud, so dry is the air, but down here it's howling relentlessly as usual. It's unpleasant to go outside in the biting cold, and for the entire morning I huddle in the comms tent with Phil, Mark, Ian, Grant, Margaret and Mila. The tent's warm with the sun on it, but still we have to put up with the violent smashing of tent canvas.

Grant's epic blog post of yesterday has won Alan Arnette's Everest Blog of the Day again. It's about the fourth time he's won this accolade on the expedition so far. He's received quite a concerned comment in response from a female admirer whom he's never met, explaining how worried she is about him. We give him some stick about this, but most of our jokes aren't suitable to print, especially Mark's.

By contrast all my post received was a frivolous comment on Facebook to a remark I made about Ian's alcohol consumption. Later in the afternoon, I receive compensation when we discover my post has been highlighted on the home page of the popular adventurers' website *ExplorersWeb*, and I've received several hundred visitors to my site as a result. I bet you never imagined life at Base Camp could be so exciting.

Happy hour becomes yet another long drinking session, and

it appears that Phil's alcohol rationing system has broken down completely. Grant arrives from an afternoon at Jamie McGuinness's camp, where he was given four glasses of 'dessert wine' (I put the phrase in inverted commas due to his description of it, which suggests he wasn't that impressed). This has made him even more garrulous than usual. He sits at one side of the table wearing a knitted red Tibetan hat with woven pigtails, making snide remarks to each member of the team in turn. He later gets his comeuppance when he burns a six-inch hole in the back of his trousers trying to warm his backside against the gas heater, much to our entertainment. The evening ends with another passionate (read 'drunken') debate, this time about global warming.

DAY 21
MEMOIRS OF A SUPERSTAR CLIMBER

Tuesday 1ˢᵗ of May, 2012 – Base Camp, Everest, Tibet

Our Sherpa team leaves early this morning to go back up to ABC. They have a tough few days ahead of them as they plan to establish camps and oxygen caches all the way up to Camp 3 at 8,300m. Words cannot express the respect I have for these guys, without whom most of us would be unable to get anywhere near the summit.

Later in the morning Phil receives our first detailed weather forecast. It predicts that the wind will begin dropping off from Friday 4th and be very light above the North Col from around the 5th to the 9th. The plan is therefore to have one more rest day here, then set off on our second rotation on Thursday. A few more days up high, followed by some rest, should hopefully put us in good shape for a summit push when the weather window comes.

We were intending to have a break from alcohol today (well, perhaps not Ian), but when Andrew Lock and Jamie McGuinness drop by again just in time for happy hour, our good intentions evaporate. The fact that we won't be walking all the way up to ABC tomorrow after all helps to persuade temperance to retire for another lie down.

For a superstar climber Andrew is remarkably relaxed in our company, leaving his ego at the door. He fits in much more easily than many of Phil's less esteemed visitors. Some of them feel the need to dominate the conversation, which often means talking about themselves. By contrast Andrew sits and listens for a lot of the time, taking an interest in other people's conversation and blending more naturally into the team, rather than behaving as an outsider.

He has plenty of stories, though, which slip out from time to time. He tells us of the time he fell into conversation with Doug Scott about climbing routes a few minutes before the legendary British climber was due on stage to give a presentation about his first ascent of the South-West Face of Everest in 1975. On that expedition he became the first Briton to climb Everest along with his climbing partner Dougal Haston. His slides were neatly arranged in the projector, but he was so determined to show Andrew a feature on the route that he ended up pulling them all out and throwing them on the floor until he found the one he wanted.

'Why the fuck doesn't he use PowerPoint?' Mark says.

I have a feeling he's missed the point of Andrew's story.

Some of Andrew's anecdotes about other climbers are more controversial, and it takes us some effort to tease them out of him. But as he intends to write a book about his climbs as soon as he's retired from mountaineering after this year's expedition, it's not for me to repeat any of them here.

DAY 22
WE'RE ALL ADULTS

Wednesday 2nd of May, 2012 – Base Camp, Everest, Tibet

It's supposed to be our last rest day before our second rotation higher up the mountain, and although the winds appeared to be dying down a little yesterday, it's howling a gale again at breakfast this morning. Phil suggests that, depending on the weather forecast that comes in later this morning, we may give ourselves another rest day before going up. It's going to be a tough ten-hour climb from Base Camp up to ABC; the last thing we want to do is make it even more exhausting by climbing into a headwind.

We have a conversation about what to do on this additional rest day which highlights the maturity of the climbers on our team

'If we do have another rest day, I'm not getting hammered again,' I tell Phil. 'I know that's the norm during rest days on Junkies' expeditions, but this time I'm not getting involved.'

'It was Ian's fault yesterday,' Mark says. 'He keeps going out and fetching more wine. I'm not going to say no after he's gone to all that trouble.'

'No, it was Grant's fault,' Ian protests.

But Grant shakes his head. 'Actually I think it was Andrew and Jamie's fault. If they hadn't turned up just in time for happy hour then I think we would have been more restrained.'

'Guys, you're all adults,' Phil says, with a disingenuous

smirk. 'You need to take responsibility for your own behaviour.'

At eleven o'clock our weather forecast arrives, and it makes us quite excited. On Friday the winds are predicted to drop off completely all the way to the summit. This should give the China Tibet Mountaineering Association an opportunity to complete the rope fixing, and our own Sherpas, who went up a couple of days ago, the chance to establish our supply lines (principally eighty oxygen bottles) at camps all the way up to 8,300m. This is the unsung donkey work which enables amateur mountaineers like me to climb in safety in a single summit push.

A huge plume of cloud as jetstream winds batter Everest's summit

We all agree there's not much point in leaving for ABC tomorrow while it's still windy, when we can leave on Friday and walk up in calm conditions. If we're feeling strong enough then we can have a short rotation of only four or five days, get up to the North Col and perhaps a little higher, then be back again resting at Base Camp by the 8th.

The forecast may predict the winds will drop at the end of the week, but there's no evidence of that happening so far. This afternoon Chomolungma wears the biggest plume of cloud I've seen yet, and clouds howl past her summit like traffic on a motorway. I decide to take a six-minute video of the summit to speed up when I get back home and demonstrate the movement of the wind, but it's so strong that my tripod keeps blowing over. The powerful blasts are perishingly cold. I have to take it in turns holding one hand on the tripod while I warm the other one up in my trouser pocket.

In the evening we're all feeling tired, and manage to subdue our alcohol consumption quite easily, even Ian. We transfer our appetite to excessive eating when Da Pasang serves up the biggest, most tender roast chicken leg I've eaten for a long time, followed by chocolate cake. My appetite has been up and down on the expedition so far, but food like this will always keep me on the right side of hunger.

DAY 23
JAMIE THE WEATHER MAN

Thursday 3rd of May, 2012 – Base Camp, Everest, Tibet

This morning is all about the weather. Phil sees members of the Adventure Peaks team passing through camp at seven o'clock this morning on their way up to ABC. There's no sign of the wind abating earlier than predicted: it's still windy as hell at Base Camp this morning, and if anything the plume on Everest's summit is even bigger than it was yesterday afternoon. Our decision to delay departure another day is looking like the right one, and no one envies Adventure Peaks the long cold day they have ahead of them.

Phil's eleven o'clock forecast from Michael Fagin of the US company *West Coast Weather* basically says the same as it did yesterday, with a period of calm expected for a few days starting from tomorrow. A little while later Andrew Lock brings Jamie McGuinness over with his laptop containing the forecast from the competing European weather company *Meteotest*. Jamie is a bit of a weather guru, and we sit in a circle in the comms tent while he reads it out and gives his interpretation. He talks in a bit more detail about cyclones and the jet stream, and the various scenarios where the models may be wrong, but essentially his forecast is the same as Phil's – although he thinks there may be a few inches of snow from the 6th onwards. Just as importantly, he doesn't see anything at the moment which may prevent a decent summit window before the end of May.

Our immediate plans are clear. We get up there, try to get above the North Col, then come back down to Base Camp again as quickly as we can. Then we rest up and wait for our summit window.

It clouds over in the afternoon, and Chomolungma hides from view as a light snow falls. The wind continues to gust; Phil begins to doubt the forecasts. But we're all keen to get out of here tomorrow after six days of doing nothing.

DAY 24
THE WORLD'S MOST ENJOYABLE
ACCLIMATISATION PROGRAMME

Friday 4th of May, 2012 – Advanced Base Camp (ABC), Everest, Tibet

At 6.30 this morning all is calm, and it looks like the weather forecasts were right after all. Phil thinks there may be a modest amount of precipitation in the afternoon, but there's no sign of the violent wind which has been our near-constant companion for the last few weeks. I set off with Mila at 7.45. Shortly after we've crossed the flat boulder plain of Base Camp and started along the narrow trail beside lateral moraine on the left-hand side of the main Rongbuk Glacier, I stop hearing her footfall behind me. I complete the rest of the ascent to ABC at my own easy pace.

There's a thin veil of cloud across the North Face of Everest, but otherwise the sky is clear, and it's pleasant walking to begin with. Phil overtakes me early on; as I start the steep plodding ascent up the side valley of the East Rongbuk, I look back to see Ian and Mark approaching behind me. Both of them had originally intended to stay down in Base Camp while the rest of us did our second rotation, but Phil persuaded them of the benefits of joining us (no doubt in part due to his concern that if Laurel and Hardy stayed in Base Camp any longer, then there may not be any alcohol left when we returned).

The temperature is very pleasant for this sort of walking. Although the sun is high, there's a chill in the air and I walk comfortably in fleece and Gore-Tex salopettes. It's easy to get into a rhythm, and a light dusting of snow has given the East Rongbuk Valley a picturesque quality. Ian overtakes me in the region of Japanese Camp but never stays very far ahead. We pass through this broad boulder-strewn area at only 9.15, and since I seem to be going well, I continue without stopping. Beyond this I pause from time to time to take two or three swigs of water, but never for longer than a minute. I pass through Interim Camp at 10.40, amazed at how well we are making time. There's no reason at all to stop for a night here once you are acclimatised. I had hoped to be able to complete today's walk in nine hours if everything went well, but now it's clear I'm going to be much quicker than that.

Approaching Changtse Base Camp

It's on the Magic Highway beyond Interim Camp that I begin to catch Ian again. While I execute the slow plod without stopping, he appears to be pausing every few metres for a breather. Only when I reach him do I realise why. He's picked up a bad cough, and every fifty metres or so he finds himself bending over to have a coughing fit. I offer him water, but he indicates that I should continue without fussing over him. A little while later I hear him coughing right behind me again, and I turn and walk back.

'Take it easy, Ian. We're making good time.'

'I think I might turn back,' he replies.

'That's not a bad idea.' I offer him water again, and ask if he wants me to call Phil on the radio for advice. But as usual for Ian, he declines all assistance.

'Don't forget, Mark is behind you. You can always discuss it with him when he catches you up.'

I leave him sitting on the moraine as I continue, but I should know from experience how tenacious he is. He soldiers on, determined to keep up with me. Despite my endless slow plod and his constant coughing fits that leave him bent double like a drunkard over a toilet bowl, he reaches camp only fifteen minutes after I do.

I stop for a snack at Changtse Base Camp, but it's cold and windy, so I rest for only five minutes for a piece of cheese and a fun-sized Mars bar before putting on my windproof jacket and continuing on my way. It has clouded over, and a light sleet is falling by the time I reach ABC at 2.45. It has taken me exactly seven hours.

'Fucking hell,' Phil says in his usual eloquent fashion as he pokes his head out of his tent. 'We weren't expecting you for another couple of hours.'

He ushers me into the kitchen tent, where all the Sherpas are sitting round after their latest carry up to the North Col. I'm given a couple of mugs of milk tea, but it takes a while for me to get my breath back, and I spend the rest of the afternoon resting in my tent. The others are also very quick. Grant and Mark arrive an hour after me, and Margaret and Mila half an hour later.

From the comfort of my tent, I hear Phil repeat, 'Fucking hell, everyone's on fire today.'

It's true, and I'm beginning to revise my opinion of what you should do on an expedition rest day. When he came over yesterday to give us his weather forecast, Jamie mentioned that it's important to get some sort of exercise every day while you're at Base Camp, and previously I would have been inclined to agree with him. But during the six days we spent at Base Camp after our first rotation, my exercise consisted of walking from sleeping tent to toilet tent to dining tent to comms tent and back again. Most of the time I've either been sitting lazily in the dining tent or lying on my back in my sleeping tent. The farthest I've walked is ten metres downwind of my tent for a pee.

In addition to this we've drunk alcohol every day, and on at least three evenings most of us have probably had the equivalent of a bottle of wine each. This isn't the best way to keep fit, but it doesn't seem to have done us any harm. In fact, Ian is the one who has picked up a cough – and he *has* been going out for short walks. It's conceivable that the wind and the dust which sneaks into your lungs make walking harmful, and cowering in our tents has actually been the healthiest option.

My regime over the last week can be best summed up as *rest and relaxation* – but at the end of it I've managed to walk seventeen kilometres and climb 1,250 vertical metres at a very high altitude in just seven hours. It's a promising sign. A better test will be to see how we perform when we go up to the North Col again in a couple of days' time. And also, of course, whether we make a similar improvement in performance when we come back for our summit push – nobody wants to peak too early.

In any case, whatever it is Phil puts in his red wine, I think I'm going to have some more of it.

DAY 25
HIGH-ALTITUDE DISCO

Saturday 5th of May, 2012 – Advanced Base Camp (ABC),
Everest, Tibet

All is white at ABC this morning. Cloudy skies and a light snow have replaced the cold and wind of our last visit. The sun is trying to peep through, which means it's very warm inside the tents, but it never quite manages to break through the cloud. There's no sign of Everest – we only know that it's up there somewhere. Our Sherpas leave at six o'clock this morning for another carry up to the col, and to move our Camp 1, which is on too steep a gradient for Phil's liking. They return at midday, and tell us that it was sweltering climbing in their down suits.

We have a rest day doing virtually nothing. It should be a peaceful afternoon, but some idiot's started a disco up here. As I lie in my tent on a glacier at 6,400m trying to get some rest, I have to listen to a pumping bass line being boomed out across ABC from a neighbouring camp. It's completely inappropriate, and I make a secret wish that the mountain gods find a way of expressing their disapproval, preferably by making a loose rock fall onto their stereo. I later revoke this curse when Phil tells me the disco belongs to the Tibetan rope-fixing team.

Where possible we've been trying to get news of other teams on the mountain using our intermittent internet connection. It's made for quite interesting reading. Things have certainly been uneventful for us compared with many other teams. The Russian

7 Summits Club team spent a night at the North Col, and described feeling trapped by the winds up there, touched as they were by the jet stream. We watched these winds from Base Camp and didn't fancy them at all. We wondered what on earth anyone was doing up there instead of staying put. It was windy enough for us down below.

On the south side of Everest it sounds like they've been experiencing even greater troubles. Apparently there's been so little snow this year that the Lhotse Face, normally a snow plod, has become loaded with rockfall. They are talking of moving the fixed ropes to a safer line, but this will involve putting them up slopes of blue ice demanding greater technical skills than many clients on Everest possess (I hesitate to call some of them 'climbers', as for a small minority of them Everest is far beyond anything they've climbed previously). All of this is just rumour to us over on the north side, but it sounds like this season on Everest is going to be an interesting one, with many lessons to be learned.

DAY 26
THE LADDER OF DEATH

Sunday 6ᵗʰ of May, 2012 – North Col, Everest, Tibet

At 6.30 this morning I'm resting inside my tent when I hear Phil shouting outside the door:

'Hey, Horrell, Meteotest were wrong about the weather.'

Although their forecasts are remarkably accurate, on this occasion the European weather forecasting service predicted there might be a lot of snowfall. We had considered spending an extra rest day at ABC if this were the case, as none of us fancied going up to the North Col in a blizzard, but it appears the weather is fine.

'It's a fucking summit day out here,' Phil says. I can sense the excitement in his voice.

We get ready promptly, have a 7.30 breakfast and leave before eight o'clock. At the very last minute, true to his character, Ian, who had been intending to rest today because of his cough, decides to join us. Being the speedster he is, he catches up with us before we reach Crampon Point. The rest of us walk at more or less the same speed and arrive together. It's much warmer than it was on our first rotation, and I don't have any problem with cold fingers this time. Once I get into a rhythm, the slow plod is easier as well. Crossing the ice plateau is a total contrast. On our first rotation a cold wind howled into our faces, but now it's fine and calm. Today the conditions are benign.

To make our climb even better, we seem to have the North

Col Wall to ourselves – many other climbers chose to go up yesterday while it was snowing. I reach the bottom of the face at about ten o'clock, but Ian, usually quite bullish, makes the wise decision to turn around. He went all the way up to the North Col on our first rotation, and the most important priority for him now is to get rid of his cough before the summit push.

(He tells us later that, as he crossed the plateau on his way back to ABC, he passed Andrew Lock coming the other way. 'Why are you coming back – isn't there any alcohol up there?' Andrew said.)

The rest of us clip into the fixed rope and begin climbing together, although Phil goes first and disappears up the wall in a puff of snow, and Mark decides to head back down again when he gets to the top of the first rope. The rest of us – me, Mila, Grant, Dorje, Margaret and Chedar – stay together all the way up, mainly because I'm leading and I'm not the world's quickest climber. I was fine walking yesterday; I can walk for as long as you like, but on steep slopes I get exhausted very quickly, and this year the route up the North Col Wall is steep, much steeper than it was when Mark, Ian and I climbed it in 2007.

We climb slowly and with frequent rests, often stopping to let a team of Sherpas pass us. By the time I reach the steep and exposed section where I turned back last time, I'm extremely tired and subjecting Mila, climbing behind me, to a cascade of obscenities, as well as less eloquent syllables such as the occasional grunt and groan.

I rest at the top. It's been unrelentingly steep for a while now, and all that remains is a short traverse along a rib of snow, followed by a tricky ladder section onto the col. I slump down in the snow where the slope has flattened, and get my breath back. Grant continues to the ladder, but the others are content to wait for me. Chedar says that it's just twenty-five minutes now.

When we catch up with Grant, he's waiting at the bottom of the ladder with his video camera, watching someone else climb up. In reality the ladder consists of two five-metre ladders tied together at a 60º angle over a deep crevasse. At the top of the ladder is a wall of ice with a narrow gully of snow leading off to the right even more steeply. This gully leading from the top of the ladder appears to be more of a problem than the ladder itself. A tangle of ropes has been attached to the wall at the top of the ladder for climbers to pull on. Two of the ropes continue up the gully to the top of the col. The gully looks hideously exposed, even without the yawning crevasse directly beneath it, and I let Grant go first to watch how it's done – he climbed up here on our first rotation.

There's a rope each side of the ladder, and he attaches his safety carabiner to one and his jumar to the other. At the top of the ladder he switches them to the two ropes leading up the gully. There are some meagre steps on this section where people have been before, but because Grant packed his axe away on his backpack when he climbed the ladder, the most secure way of climbing up is by pulling hard on one of the ropes with his jumar. I follow behind and make good progress, but just at the top of the gully I chance to glance down, and I'm sickened by the exposure. The only way I'm going to get down that thing, I think to myself, is by abseiling, but the angle is awkward and the tangle of ropes above the ladder may cause a problem. One thing is for sure – I'm not looking forward to going back down again.

But for now I'm on the North Col, having found it an order of magnitude harder than when I climbed up here five years ago. Snow and ice conditions differ from year to year, and the route up the wall is never the same. This year the route is much more direct. I make my way slowly along the broad ledge of snow that is the North Col campsite, Camp 1. Tents line both sides of the path which leads through camp. There are probably about fifty tents here, and our camping space is somewhere in the middle. I see Phil, who has been waiting here for an hour or so, and Andrew Lock, who overtook us on the way up and is busy pitching his tent.

It's about 1.30; the sky has clouded over slightly and a light snow is falling. We are all very tired, and any thought of walking a little higher up the North Ridge is far from our minds. Even walking to the end of the campsite and beyond, to see the summit ridge in touching distance and the view across to the south side, is pointless now that everything is hidden from view. I looked upon these sights five years ago, and they convinced me that one day I might be able to do this climb myself and stand on the roof of the world. We hope to see them again when we come back up on our summit push.

We rest beside the tents and enjoy a light snack. Margaret, an Australian herself, provokes collective groans when she asks to be photographed with Andrew, Australia's most celebrated high-altitude mountaineer.

'Groupie, groupie!' cries Phil.

Andrew takes a photo of the seven of us from the Altitude Junkies team who have made it up here, and then we begin to think about heading down again.

'I'm going to have to abseil down that ladder section,' I say.

Phil shakes his head. 'You can't. The rope's too tight. It's a handrail only.'

'Are you serious?'

Mila and Margaret seem to be as nervous about descending it as I am. Margaret has Chedar as her personal Sherpa, and Phil agrees to guide me down it while Dorje guides Mila. We say our goodbyes to Andrew, who is spending a night here before doing a carry up to Camp 2 tomorrow, and walk slowly back to the top of the wall. While we wait above for some Indian climbers to descend the ladder section, Phil offers me some useful advice for descending fixed ropes using a two-handed technique he calls *hand wrapping*. I've been taught how to *arm wrap*, a technique which involves wrapping the rope around my arm as I descend. It provides safety by locking my arm in the rope in the event of a fall, but it doesn't give me any control – nothing to reduce the likelihood of me falling in the first place, which in this steep, exposed gully is a distinct possibility. Hand wrapping, by contrast, involves gripping the rope firmly with gloved hands, rather than wrapping it around the arms, and using the upward hand as the dominant point of safety.

Phil makes his way down the gully in front of me, shouting up instructions as he goes. He makes it look easy, but I have to swallow my fear as I wait above him, staring down the gully. He gets to the bottom and it's my turn. I carefully lower myself down some vertiginous footholds, and clip into the rope at the top of the gully. As I do so I realise Phil's hand wrapping technique gives me a great deal of stability. Instead of loosely relying on the rope to hold my fall, I'm using it to control where I go, and I'm much more stable. I even have the confidence to unclip my carabiner halfway down the gully when I realise I'm clipped into the wrong rope. At the top of the ladder there is a step of faith where I have to face into the ice wall and step down without being able to see where my foot is going, but once onto the ladder things are easy.

Phil and Grant are waiting at the bottom of the ladder with another group of climbers who are on their way up. They still have a while to wait. Dorje and Mila descend together smoothly, but above them Margaret is finding it more difficult. Unlike us, she's decided to face into the slope, but she has much shorter legs, so her descent is a series of steps of faith instead of just one. But Chedar climbs below and guides her feet with care and expertise, and we all reach the bottom of the ladder safely.

There remains the question of the rest of the North Col Wall. Although we've descended the hardest bit, many steep and exposed sections remain. On our previous visit I found four of them steep enough to warrant abseiling, but having hand wrapped down the gully I'm damned if I'm going to abseil down any of the other bits. Armed with Phil's technique I carefully make my way down. Although it's tiring I feel remarkably stable. I'm very slow, but Phil decides to keep an eye on me all the way down. It's a big confidence boost when I reach the bottom. I feel like I've learned something today, and I've improved as a climber thanks to Phil – although I know purists will argue that descending a fixed rope isn't proper climbing.

We wait for each other at the foot of the wall, and make our way across the ice plateau together, reaching ABC at around four o'clock after an eight-hour round trip. All our Sherpas are crowded into the kitchen tent and they offer us refuge. Pemba gives us a plate of chips, which we greedily wolf down, along with a few mugs of tea. It's been a tiring but rewarding day.

DAY 27
EAST RONGBUK MONOTONY

Monday 7th of May, 2012 – Base Camp, Everest, Tibet

Phil has some momentous news at breakfast, which has been emailed to his satellite phone by his wife Trish. One of the biggest expedition teams on the south side of Everest, Russell Brice's Himex team, are quitting the mountain because of the danger of rockfall on the Lhotse Face (we later learn that even more hazardous conditions in the Khumbu Icefall were their main concern). It's big news. There are usually hundreds of summits on the south side every year, but if the Himex team has pulled out then it seems likely other teams will follow. It's still early in the season and there's plenty of time for conditions to improve, but already it's looking like a bad year on the south side. By contrast here on the north everything seems to be going smoothly, with no real dramas.

We're tired, tired, tired this morning, but the thought of another rest day up here at ABC is about as appealing as a dinner date with Simon Cowell and Piers Morgan. One by one after breakfast we drag our weary feet out of camp and begin heading down the East Rongbuk Glacier. I leave at nine o'clock behind Mark, Ian, Grant and Mila. I walk so slowly that I don't expect to see any of them before Base Camp. The terrain is very difficult for tired feet – never flat, with loose stones and boulders to trip me up at every moment – real ankle-twisting stuff. The scenery is now very monotonous, with many sections that seem to continue without variation for hours. Chief among these is the part between Changtse Base Camp and Interim Camp, up and down and up and down over rough, loose rocks. It doesn't help when I meet a herd of yaks coming the other way on a narrow section which ascends steeply from Changtse Base Camp. There's no space to pass, and I can't scamper down the slope because of the risk of rocks being dislodged, so I have to scramble hastily up some loose boulders. This knocks the stuffing out of me for a good few minutes.

Descending the Magic Highway from ABC

I pass Grant a little later, who has stopped to talk to Jamie. Several of Jamie's ABC trekkers also pass on their way up. The other really tedious bit is the dry dusty desert section below Interim Camp, where a wind whips up, sucking dust into my lungs. Phil catches me up on a section where the trail cuts across an ice lake. Below this, the scenery is more variable, and I feel like I'm making progress rather than being stuck in a time warp where every footstep seems to get me nowhere. I reach the end of the East Rongbuk valley, where it meets the main Rongbuk Glacier, and complete the flatter section back to Base Camp in a little under an hour.

I reach the haven of Base Camp, home again, at two o'clock. This time Phil is there to welcome me with Lhasa Beer rather than Red Bull, but unlike the first rotation, when our return to Base Camp signalled a bit of a drinking session, today feels different. We're more tired. It's cloudy, windy and cold at Base Camp, and I have a bad cough. I feel sure it's from all the dust I've swallowed. I have to take a nap in the afternoon, and I even decline the red wine I'm offered at happy hour. Da Pasang cooks another beautifully tender chicken breast for dinner, but I have a coughing fit on my way back to my tent and end up bringing much of it back up again. Still, at least we have a few rest days to recover now, and it's always a great feeling when I climb inside my huge down sleeping bag at Base Camp and let my head hit the pillow.

DAY 28
'VISITING THE MONASTERY'

Tuesday 8th of May, 2012 – Base Camp, Everest, Tibet

We have more news from the south side at breakfast, when Grant decides to crank up his laptop and check all the Everest blogs. We learn that although one of the larger teams, Himex, has pulled out, conditions on the Lhotse Face have now stabilised, and people are going back up again. It seems there will be summits on the south side after all. At lunch Phil explains the real reason why they're having such a disastrous time on the south compared with what we're experiencing here on the north.

'Dorje tells me it's because with all those 350 western climbers at Base Camp this year there's going to be a hell of a lot more people having sex, and the mountain gods don't like it.'

It's certainly true that sort of behaviour isn't happening in the Junkies' camp, or at least not that I'm aware of.

Today's weather forecast states there may be high winds above 6,000m until the 15th, which means we'll be sitting tight here at Base Camp for a week or more. I mention that I might go for a walk down to the Rongbuk Monastery in a couple of days' time.

'Oh, yeah?' Phil says. 'We know what that means.'

He mimes someone drinking. In his parlance, 'going to the monastery' is a euphemism for walking down to the tented Tibetan Village and getting drunk in one of the teahouses. I look across at Ian.

'I think I might join you, Mark,' he says.

Everybody roars with laughter. Ian has been on antibiotics for the last few days to try and shake off his cough, and this has meant staying off the booze. In a couple of days' time he will have completed his course and will be able to drink again.

The slightly frustrating thing is, I did genuinely mean I wanted to visit the monastery, but nobody believes me.

DAY 29
LOCK UNLOCKED

Wednesday 9th of May, 2012 – Base Camp, Everest, Tibet

Another rest day at Base Camp, and once again we're back into the routine of having a leisurely eight o'clock breakfast and then doing odd tasks such as showering, shaving and washing clothes.

We try to get more information about the south side dramas, but there doesn't seem to be any news to report today. If anything, conditions on the Lhotse Face seem to be getting safer and summits are looking ever more likely, which makes the decision of Himex to pull out early all the more baffling.

At eleven o'clock Crazy Chris comes over with a box of Jaffa Cakes left behind by a member of his team who decided Everest wasn't for him. His visit coincides with Phil's eleven o'clock weather forecast, which predicts the high winds will continue until the 16th, but may drop off thereafter. We have now prepared ourselves for a long wait here at Base Camp.

At four o'clock Andrew Lock arrives – quite coincidentally, I'm sure – just as we're sitting down for happy hour. He's returned from completing a carry up to Camp 2, and Phil invites him for dinner as we work our way through several Lhasa Beers. He tells us the China Tibet Mountaineering Association (CTMA) have definitely fixed ropes as high as Camp 3 at 8,300m.

Apparently there's not much space left on the various ledges that form Camp 2. Andrew tells us that our Sherpas raced past him *on juice* (in other words, they were using bottled oxygen). Although they like to remind Phil they can climb without it, when his Sherpas use oxygen it makes him happy because it means they are well treated. We need strong Sherpas for our summit push, so anything that makes these essential load carries easier is a good thing. Andrew also reports that Asian Trekking took over our camping space at Camp 1, which is bad etiquette and is bound to annoy our sirdar Dorje.

Phil and Andrew get more talkative as the evening progresses, and start reminiscing about climbers they have known. Andrew hints about having a dislike for Alan Hinkes, the well-known British mountaineer who is still the only Briton to have climbed all fourteen 8,000m peaks. We know he intends to retire and write a book after this expedition, so we don't push him for details of anything he may be saving for it, but in the end he can't help himself.

'All right then, do you want to hear my Hinkes story?' he suddenly says.

We all cheer.

He tells us about his ascent of Nanga Parbat in 1998, when Alan Hinkes was his climbing partner, and it reminds me of the controversial first ascent of K2 in 1954. Nobody can be certain what happened on that occasion, but one popular interpretation is that on the evening before their successful summit assault, the Italians Achille Compagnoni and Lino Lacedelli denied shelter in their tent to their teammates Walter Bonatti and the Pakistani porter Mahdi, who had brought up vital oxygen supplies. Bonatti and Mahdi had to spend a night in the open, huddling together on a precipitous snow slope as the wind battered against them. Compagnoni and Lacedelli became the first men to climb K2, but Mahdi had severe frostbite, and the consequences could easily have been worse.

In Andrew's case he and a Pakistani high-altitude porter (or HAP, as they are known) broke trail through deep snow all the way from their high camp to the summit. Every time they stopped for a breather, Hinkes and a group of Korean climbers hung back and waited for them, refusing to take their turn breaking trail.

After reaching the summit late, the climbers descended in darkness and Andrew overshot camp. He looked up and saw the torches of his companions go out as they found their tents and crawled into their sleeping bags, but nobody came to find him. Unable to locate the camp he was forced to bivouac out in the open and endure a freezing cold night. At first light he discovered he was only a few metres from camp, and inside his own tent he found Hinkes wrapped up snugly in both his and Andrew's sleeping bags.

At the end of his story Andrew leans back and says with a wry grin: 'And that's the reason I hate the bugger so much.'

It's as though it happened so long ago that it's no more than a funny story now.

I look forward to reading his book, which Grant says should be called *Lock Unlocked*. (It was eventually published in Australia and New Zealand in 2014 with the more mundane but descriptive title *Summit 8000*. Elsewhere it was published as *Master of Thin Air*, which makes him sound a bit like a character from a fantasy novel.)

DAY 30
RUSSIAN HOSPITALITY

Thursday 10th of May, 2012 – Base Camp, Everest, Tibet

At breakfast this morning Margaret tells us about her Everest summit day last year on the south side.

'Remember when I dropped my glove and you caught it?' she says to Phil. 'I still don't know how you did that!'

'It's because I have superhuman powers,' is Phil's reply.

Five of them were climbing up to the South Summit in the dark, with Margaret at the front and Phil at the back, when Margaret's glove came off and was taken by the wind. Had she lost it then, it would have meant the end of her summit attempt at best, and severe frostbite at worst. But she shouted, and Phil stuck out his hand and caught it.

'To be fair,' Mark says, 'if you were a superhero and your superhuman power was glove catching, then you'd be a bit pissed off!'

Phil's comment ends up backfiring, and we spend the rest of the morning calling him Glovecatcher Man.

After lunch, Phil, Mark, Ian and Grant decide to walk across the boulders to Jamie McGuinness's camp and accept Andrew Lock's reciprocal offer of afternoon beers. To prevent an invasion, and because I don't feel comfortable drinking that early in the afternoon, I decide to stay in camp, have a snooze and read a bit of my book.

Everything is set for an uneventful afternoon. Chomolungma

clouds over and the wind picks up. By the time I leave my tent for four o'clock happy hour, it's really quite cold and putting on my down clothing doesn't seem like overdoing it. No sooner have I joined Mila and Margaret in the dining tent than Ian bursts in and says the Russian 7 Summits Club team are having a party tonight and everyone in Base Camp is invited. The 7 Summits Club have learned that we have a Russian on our team, and Ian has been sent on a special mission to fetch Mila.

The Russian camp is located at the farthest end of Base Camp, directly underneath the tall bank of terminal moraine at the snout of the Rongbuk Glacier. They have a huge white dome with chairs around the edge and a table in the middle, which seems to contain as much free food and drink as everyone in Base Camp can manage. It's extremely generous of them, and there's a nice gesture when their leader Alex Abramov stands up and makes a speech to say we should all be prepared to help each other out on the mountain and not compete.

My companions make great efforts to circulate with other teams, but for the most part I'm content to stand at the edge and watch. There are a good fifty or sixty people. Most of the Russians sport sizeable beards and facial whiskers, and many of the other Europeans seem to have craggy faces that look like they've been hewn from a cliff using an ice axe. Many people have quite severe sun and wind burn, too; halfway through the evening it occurs to me that I've never been in a room with so many ugly people. If there was a mirror then I have no doubt I would count myself among them.

There are a number of Australians, and Andrew and Margaret discover a few fans who ask them to pose for photographs. Mila acts as interpreter for a couple of portly Chechen climbers who are keen to talk to Andrew. All I can make out are the words 'Ah – Andrew Lock, Andrew Lock!' repeated in booming Russian accents. There is enough to keep me amused without getting too involved in conversation, and when some of the more hirsute mountaineers find their way onto a makeshift dance floor, it's considerably more entertaining than *Strictly Come Dancing*.

We take advantage of Russian hospitality for three hours, but back in the Junkies' camp Da Pasang and Pemba have been busy cooking another delicious chicken breast and chips, so at 6.30 we pull ourselves away and return for dinner. One or two tins of Lhasa Beer seem to have found their way into deep pockets, and we toast Russian warmth and generosity on our return.

DAY 31
THE TIBETAN VILLAGE

Friday 11th of May, 2012 – Base Camp, Everest, Tibet

Feeling a little guilty about our over-indulgence yesterday, Ian and I decide to get a bit of exercise this morning. We wander down the road to the lower part of the Rongbuk Valley. About an hour's walk below Base Camp is a settlement of about sixty tented souvenir shops arranged around a square, known as the Tibetan Village.

Just before we reach it, we find a small gompa perched high on a rocky outcrop above the valley. This is the Zarongbuk Monastery, an outlier of the main Rongbuk Monastery further down the valley. When we came here five years ago, Ian and I had the surreal experience of being pulled down a trapdoor by a group of boisterous Tibetan pilgrim women, and found ourselves in an underground crypt where a monk was lighting butter lamps. Today the place is deserted, and we spend a few minutes exploring its compound. Tiny monastery buildings, prayer flags and chortens are spread out among a tumble of sheltered rocks, with Everest as a backdrop. It's tucked away off the dusty road and is very peaceful given its location next to a major tourist attraction, with busloads of sightseers driving past from time to time.

Down in the Tibetan Village we stop for a Coke in one of the tented teahouses. The wind has dropped and it's swelteringly hot as we sit and sip. The Tibetan teahouse owner tries to converse with us in broken English, but we don't get very far. There's a post office here; we stop for Ian to write postcards to his nephews. He buys too many, and offers some of them to me.

'Are you sure you don't want any postcards, Mark?'

'Postcards?' I reply. 'This is the 21st century.'

I sit on a rock and wait for him, tapping away on my iPhone, and posting my geographical location to the social networking site Foursquare. I post a photo of Ian to Facebook, which I took with the camera on my phone.

Everest from the Tibetan village

It takes us about an hour to return up the hill to Base Camp. Ian, incapable of walking slowly, sets a vigorous pace while I linger behind, sweating in the hot sun. Luckily the China Winds are behind us, cancelling out the effect of the prevailing winds which otherwise would have blown a large quantity of silver dust into our faces. It's been a good three-hour workout, and we get back to Base Camp at around midday.

Back in camp Phil is very excited about the latest weather

forecast. 'We should be able to summit on the 20th or 21st,' he says.

This means we have another two or three rest days before we head back up the mountain. After lunch he gives us an explanation of how we'll be splitting our six oxygen bottles among the three high camps. We start on our first bottle between Camps 1 and 2, and continue using it to sleep on while we're at Camp 2. A second bottle will get us from Camp 2 to Camp 3, and we set out from Camp 3 on our summit push with two bottles each. The second bottle should have enough oxygen remaining to get us through the night when we return from our summit attempt, and a fifth bottle will get us back down to Camp 1. We each have a sixth bottle to use as a spare in an emergency.

Phil gives a practical demonstration on the dinner table, using espresso cups to signify the bottles, but it's a bit complicated to follow. I certainly need a strong coffee to get my head round it, and I suspect he may have been smoking something more potent than coffee beans while we were away.

Discussing our summit push doesn't exactly fill me with anticipation. On the contrary, it makes me feel nervous. There are so many little things to consider, but common sense and experience will help us do most of them mechanically. Chongba will be climbing Everest for the thirteenth time, so I'm hoping he'll be able to help me out with the oxygen routine.

DAY 32
HOW NOT TO WRITE AN EXPEDITION DISPATCH

Saturday 12th of May, 2012 – Base Camp, Everest, Tibet

A day of minor setbacks which conspire to leave me feeling slightly down. In the morning I decide to read Grant's blog post from yesterday, whose title hints that he has some insight into the whereabouts of Sandy Irvine's body, something that has been intriguing people ever since George Mallory's body was found on slabs below the First Step in 1999. Mallory was believed to be carrying a camera when he disappeared with Irvine in 1924, but it wasn't found on his body, so many people now believe Irvine was carrying it. They hope that if the camera can be found and its film developed, it will confirm once and for all whether the pair of them reached the summit twenty-nine years before Hillary and Tenzing. Personally I believe Irvine must have fallen all the way down the North Face – the rope around Mallory's waist was broken – and his body is now crushed somewhere deep inside the Rongbuk Glacier. It'll emerge at the glacier snout many years hence, by which time the camera won't be in very good condition. Even if they did get to the summit, they didn't get back alive, and getting back alive is a vital part of any climb.

But despite the title, Grant's blog post isn't about that. It turns out to be the most depressing rant about all the ways he might die on summit day, and how every moment spent in the *death zone* (deep voice and evil laugh) is slowly killing him. He writes of how it's so cold up there that if he takes his gloves off he might lose his fingers 'for ever' (cue loud organ music and more evil laughter) – which suggests there are some ways of losing your fingers and getting them back again. He talks about how he might fall down the North Face and die instantly because the thin air of high altitude gives him the mind of a seven to ten-year-old boy.

I've been reading the post out to Mark in my best husky Hollywood movie trailer voice, and at this point he interrupts.

'But how does that work – how can a lack of oxygen make him more intelligent?'

We both agree that Grant should have to pay some sort of forfeit for writing such a depressing post just a few days before our summit push.

Then at eleven o'clock Phil brings the latest weather forecast, which suggests the winds will pick up again on the 21st. This would leave the 18th, 19th and 20th as the only possible – and narrowest – of summit windows.

Crazy Chris comes over and confirms the ropes have only been fixed as high as 8,300m. The rumour is that some impatient teams went over to the CTMA to complain the ropes weren't being fixed quickly enough, to which the leader of the rope-fixing team responded in a fit of resentment by immediately ordering his rope fixers down from the mountain. We're now told the last bit of the route will be fixed on the 18th and 19th, narrowing the window even more, and opening up the scary possibility that everyone on the north side of the mountain will be trying to summit on the 20th.

Phil then asks me if I would mind sharing a tent with Grant on our summit push.

'Not at all,' I reply, 'as long as he agrees to keep the conversation light.'

Luckily Grant's blog post was written for dramatic effect, presumably for the benefit of readers back home who aren't worrying about him as much as they should be. He's nowhere near as pessimistic in real life as his writing style suggests.

But today isn't all bad news. In the afternoon our Sherpa crew return from their long, exhausting stint at ABC and above, establishing all our supplies right the way up to 8,300m. This means the only remaining pieces of the jigsaw are the fixed rope to the summit and a decent weather window – and there's the rub.

Later in the afternoon I look out of my tent and see Chongba emerging from behind the dining tent. He greets me with the most cheerful grin you could possibly imagine, and although he's probably been having a celebratory beer or two, the sight of my summit-day Sherpa looking so buoyant and optimistic erases any lingering depression caused by this morning's other developments.

In the morning Mila and Margaret walked down to the Tibetan Village, and on the way they bumped into the famous Russian explorer-priest we first talked about in Tingri, who was apparently hoping to place a cross on the summit. We hadn't heard anything more about this story until we went to the Russian party the other day and saw the cross standing proudly outside their dome tent. It was an impressive thing, about six feet tall, made from wood and standing on a sturdy platform. It won't be easy to carry it up – or back down again. The priest confirmed to Mila that he hopes to carry the cross to the summit and leave it there, but the good news is that he's sensitive enough to realise he needs to apply for permission from the Chinese government in order to do so. The chances of a Communist government allowing a religious symbol to be placed on the summit of their highest mountain seem about as good as me making it up there without oxygen, blindfolded and walking on my hands. I think Mila can rest assured that Chomolungma is not going to be defiled in this way.

Later in the evening Grant atones for his blog hell. He tries to lighten the mood by describing an incident that happened when he was a student in Dunedin, New Zealand. He tried to urinate his name into the snow on the main street while police were driving past. He was arrested and spent a night in the cells. I ask if it gave him a lifelong grudge against the police, as such incidents seem to do for many otherwise sensible people.

'Hell no, it was my own stupid fault. They were only doing their job.'

There's a lesson in there somewhere for the rest of us, if it's only to give Grant a wide berth when he stops on some snowy ledge during our summit push.

DAY 33
AN EMERGENCY MEETING

Sunday 13th of May, 2012 – Base Camp, Everest, Tibet

We have a full camp once again. Yesterday our superstar Sherpa team came down from the mountain after two heroic load carries up to 8,300m. They were tired, and spent most of the day resting; poor Dorje has injured his leg, which means he may not be able to join us on the summit push.

Although we're not due to go up again for another two days at the earliest, I nurse a feeling of nervous tension for much of the morning. The best way to ease this anxiety is not to think about the climb as a whole – that I am planning to climb Everest, the highest mountain in the world, with a rich history of deadly incidents – but to take each day as it comes, that today all I need to do is walk from A to B, then rest. It's the same with any big project. There's no point getting intimidated by the scale of the whole thing; just break it down into manageable chunks. As the Tibetans might say, if you're going to eat a whole yak you can only do it one bite at a time.

My anxiety is eased when I see Chongba again while I'm brushing my teeth outside the tent. He still has that broad grin on his face. He's climbed Everest twelve times, but never from the north. This will be his first time, just as it was for both of us when we climbed Manaslu together last year. He's brimming with confidence, and I realise I'm a lucky man. With Chongba to look after me how can I fail? I certainly can't let him down, that's for sure.

Yet this growing apprehension in the pit of my stomach remains for much of the morning. I try to take my mind off it by writing a blog post, but the post is about Mallory and Somervell climbing up to the North Col, and it focuses my mind on the task instead of easing it. Phil is nervous, too, for a different reason. As I sit and type in the comms tent, he's waiting for the eleven o'clock weather forecast which may change our plans, but it never arrives. It will be good to get moving.

Much later, at eight o'clock in the evening after we've had dinner, I'm tucked up in my sleeping bag reading by the light of my Kindle when I hear Phil wandering around camp. He shouts through every tent in turn: the weather forecast has just come in and it's very important, so important that we all have to get up immediately and discuss it. It's not very often a man likes to be dragged from his bed to be given bad news, but Phil is only doing what he has to do.

I put all my down clothing back on and climb out of my tent to attend an emergency meeting in the kitchen tent. All of the Sherpas are there too. Everybody is filled with anticipation, sharing nervous glances.

The bad news is that the summit window is now even shorter. The jet stream will move back in again on the 20th, our intended summit day, producing winds of 50mph. Since it's likely the ropes to the summit won't be fixed before the 18th, the 19th is now our one and only opportunity. It means that if we want to keep to the same schedule, with a rest day at ABC on the way up, we must leave tomorrow. This suggestion produces as much excitement as a request for somebody to empty the toilet barrel. There's a silent groan. We unanimously agree that we'll stay here in Base Camp tomorrow, as planned, and that we'll have to push on through ABC without a rest day. This will make things tougher for us, but we all believe it's possible.

My biggest concern is what is technically termed a *clusterfuck* on the North-East Ridge. If the 19th is the only possible summit window, then doesn't it mean every climber in Base Camp will be going for the summit that day? I have no idea how many climbers can be on the summit ridge at any one time before it becomes unsafe, so I ask those with more experience for their thoughts.

All of the Sherpas remain silent, and I'm not that surprised. Apart from Chedar, none of them have summited from the north, and they'll take whatever opportunity they can. They're all keen to go on the 19th but they don't want to influence our decision, so they keep quiet. Phil says that over 300 people went for the summit on the same day on the south side last year; although they didn't all summit, there was no accident. Margaret makes the point that a calm day with many climbers is much safer than a day with high winds and few climbers. Weather poses our biggest danger, not people.

There is one alternative to the 19th, but it's much less certain. There might be another summit window a week later, but we have no information about this yet. It may happen, it may not; it would be a roll of the dice, and we all believe the narrow sliver of a window on the 19th represents our best chance of success.

The more I think about it the more I realise that we have no choice. I'm not a gambler, and it's not a decision I can take to roll those dice when a realistic opportunity lies before me. I return to my tent for some sleep, knowing that the first few lines of our summit push story have now been written.

DAY 34
THE SUMMIT MINDSET

Monday 14ᵗʰ of May, 2012 – Base Camp, Everest, Tibet

A morning of blogging; we spend the first few hours of today sending out messages to friends, family and followers. We have an early meeting in the comms tent with the Sherpas, and Phil confirms the schedule we agreed last night.

Our main concern is the number of climbers who may be going for the summit on the 19th, so Phil asks the Sherpas to talk to their friends in other teams to see if they can discover what their plans are. Although nothing is certain, we don't think everyone on the north side will be going on the same day as we are. Some, such as the big Indian and Chinese teams, look like they may try to follow right behind the rope fixers on the 18th, and some just won't be ready for this early summit window. Others aren't aware the forecast has changed, and some like Jamie intend to hold out for the hope of a later window. Whatever, for us it's now just one foot in front of the other, and the rest is in the hands of the mountain gods.

At lunchtime Phil insists we drink beer. This means an early-afternoon snooze. I wake up at three o'clock and pack the very small quantity of things I need to take up to ABC tomorrow. I think about a leg stretch up a nearby hillside, but exercise is a double-edged sword here because of the wind. The chance of swallowing dust is high, and the last thing any of us wants to do now is pick up a bad cough. I don't know whether I will be fit enough: I hope so, but if I'm not then a leg stretch up a hill this afternoon is neither here nor there.

At least I have the determination. And then there's Chongba, who doesn't want me to flag now. My nervousness of yesterday seems to have faded, replaced by a kind of fatalism. I know I will do my best, but there are a million other factors out of my control. Only the ticking of the clock will reveal the answer this time next week.

DAY 35
THE SUMMIT PUSH BEGINS

*Tuesday 15th of May, 2012 – Advanced Base Camp (ABC),
Everest, Tibet*

Our summit push begins with an early start. First light is about
4.45, and my Base Camp routine has usually been to wake up at
5.15 and snooze in my bag for a couple of hours until the sun
hits the tent at 7.30. Because we want as much rest as possible
when we reach ABC, we've agreed to have a 5.30 breakfast
today, so that anyone who wants to make an early start can do
so.

I leave at 6.20, shortly after Phil and Grant, and am surprised
to catch them up a few minutes later. It's quite cold. I start out
with freezing fingers and toes, but they soon warm up as we
walk in leisurely fashion alongside the main Rongbuk Glacier,
and it's pleasant walking again. We have our clearest view yet of
Everest and the peaks of the Khumbu beyond the West Ridge.
The weather forecast warned us to expect strong winds, but
there's only the occasional gust. Better still, the prevailing winds
would usually be in our faces on our climb up to ABC, but much
to our relief the wind is behind us instead.

Normal service is resumed when the path steepens as we
branch off into the East Rongbuk Valley and Phil speeds off into
the distance ahead of us. I find myself walking in front of Grant,
and continue my non-stop high-altitude plod as I did last time,
through the dusty desert below Interim Camp, and along the

ankle-twisting moraine of the Magic Highway above it. There are a few people plodding up the moraine today, but not the crowds we feared. Much of the ice which the path used to cross at Changtse Base Camp is starting melt, and I have to take care walking past it. But this is a sign the mountain is getting warmer, which bodes well for our summit day, when frostbite is a risk.

I continue without pausing, but on the higher section of the Magic Highway above Changtse Base Camp I feel myself flagging and running out of energy, so I sit down for a piece of cheese and a Snickers bar. Here I have a funny encounter with a couple of Europeans of unidentified nationality. They have been catching me up slowly, and when they pass me sitting on my rock one of them stops to ask me what time I left Base Camp.

'About 6.30,' I reply. 'It usually takes me seven hours from Base Camp to ABC.'

'Oh.' He seems pleased. 'And you are the last in your group?'

'No, in fact I think I'm the first.'

'Oh,' he says again. This seems to please him even more.

I don't ask him how long it has taken him because I don't really care – I'm not racing anyone, and the important thing at this stage is to conserve energy, but he reminds me of another climber we met at Base Camp who has produced a website about his Everest climb in an attempt to get sponsorship. The website focuses on his fitness regime rather than his climbing record, and one of his claims is that he's a member of two gyms. This made us laugh when we were looking at the website on Grant's laptop at Base Camp; we couldn't imagine how this could possibly help you get sponsorship for a mountaineering expedition, but many people who attempt Everest are competitive athletes rather than mountaineers, and they see it as a hard physical challenge rather than a climb. I'm not a member of any gyms and never have been. Hopefully it won't hamper my chances.

Anyway, unfortunately for my new ultra-competitive European friend, my little snack gives me a renewed burst of energy. I steam past him again and arrive into ABC at one o'clock. Our poor Sherpas, who arrived only a little before me, are having to re-pitch the tents because the Tibetan kitchen crew put them up the wrong way round. No-one is critical though – they were trying to be helpful, and have been up here at ABC looking after our camp for twenty-five days now.

They usher me into the kitchen tent and give me milk tea. Phil is very bullish, some might say over-confident. He has spoken to the Tibetan rope fixers and learned they will probably be fixing the rest of the route on the 17th. This is good news – it might mean that the eager-beaver climbers will try to summit on the 18th.

'Dude, it's in the bag,' he says to me. 'I spoke to Chongba. He only got to the North Col on his two previous climbs this side, but not this time.'

I interpret this to mean my summit attempt is in the bag, rather than the team's as a whole. Chongba will be with me on summit day, so whether or not he reaches the summit largely depends on me.

'I hope he'll get above the North Col, but it's not in the bag. It's never in the bag till we've got up and down,' I reply.

Phil knows this, but there's no doubt his enthusiasm is infectious, and it does leave me feeling more confident. But there's still a long way to go.

I retire to my tent and begin preparing my things for tomorrow's climb to the North Col. It's going to be a much harder day getting up that steep wall with a big pack.

We all crowd into the kitchen tent again for dinner because the dining tent is damp. For some reason Margaret has completely lost her voice and is having to mime conversation. It's all a bit comical whenever she wants to speak, like some silent Buster Keaton movie. Phil says it always happens to her on the summit push, but it's odd that it didn't happen last time we were up here.

I've been wondering how I'm going to put up with Grant's chatter at the higher camps; I'm not much of a talker on summit pushes, and Grant is rather more garrulous.

'Phil, whatever you gave Margaret at Base Camp can you give it to Grant, too?' I say.

DAY 36
BOTTLENECK ON THE NORTH COL WALL

Wednesday 16th of May, 2012 – Camp 1, North Col, Everest, Tibet

We may have ascended 1,200m of rocky terrain in just a few hours, but yesterday was the easy part of our summit push. The real climbing, five days of it, begins today.

We all agree that the North Col Wall is best tackled with a companion. I wanted to leave early this morning to give myself as much rest as possible at Camp 1, and Mark wanted to leave a little later, so we agreed to compromise and start at 9.30. Mila comes with us and we eventually leave at 9.45. No sooner have we climbed up the big mound of rubbly moraine above our camp to get onto the main trail than Mark realises he's set off without his ice axe. This is one item he can't do without, and he goes back down to get it, but as Mila and I have been kept waiting for fifteen minutes already we decide to continue without him.

The 150m of ascent up the moraine to Crampon Point is the most exhausting yet, highly demoralising considering how far we still have to climb on this summit push. This is mainly because of the extra kit we have to carry. I've tried to travel as light as possible, but even so all the essentials add up – sleeping bag, sleeping mat, down suit, radio, two pairs of down mitts, two head torches with spare batteries, snow goggles, first aid kit, pee bottle, toilet paper, two cameras with spare batteries, and water bottles. These are the things in my pack; then there are the other items of weighty equipment I'm wearing, such as the huge *La Sportiva* mountaineering boots, crampons, harness, carabiners and jumar. Tomorrow I'll be able to ditch the bulky Gore-Tex I currently have on and wear my down suit the rest of the way up, but a 4kg oxygen cylinder and mask will replace the Gore-Tex in my pack.

We reach Crampon Point exhausted (or I do, at any rate), but when I look at my watch I realise we've made pretty good time. It's only eleven o'clock. There are lots of other climbers here getting cramponed up, though most of them seem to be Sherpas. It's clear quite a lot of people have decided this is a good summit window, though thankfully by no means everyone in Base Camp.

We set off across the ice plateau. I take it very slowly, and we often have to stop to let Sherpas past. We rest briefly at the foot of the wall before clipping in and starting out on the first bit of real climbing. We agree to take it very easy, with frequent stops if we need them, but often we have to stop to let Sherpas past anyway. Although it's busy on the wall today, Sherpas are not the problem because they move more quickly than anyone else on the mountain, even when carrying heavy loads. They're not the ones who cause bottlenecks. Early on in the climb we stop to let a Chinese girl and her team of three Sherpas past, all moving faster than we are; but later she slows down and causes a queue.

Mila and I continue slowly and take a long rest on a snow balcony about halfway up, just before the slope becomes steeper and stays that way for most of the remaining climb. It's on this section we reach the bottleneck. There must be twenty or thirty other climbers ahead of us and no suitable place to overtake. We have no option but to proceed at their pace. The Chinese girl appears to be at the front, but a couple of very slow American climbers are ahead of us too.

One man is circumventing the bottleneck by not clipping in to the fixed rope, and climbing beside people instead. He is using two sticks instead of an ice axe, which means he has no way of arresting should he fall. The slope is way too steep for poles and he has to hold them halfway down the shaft. In some of the steeper parts he really struggles and makes the bottleneck worse. People climbing behind him get nervous. Some climbers refuse to use fixed ropes because they regard it as cheating, but doing so on a busy mountain like this puts not only himself in danger but other climbers as well. Compounding the danger by using walking sticks instead of an ice axe is extremely selfish.

By now Phil has caught up with us, and he puts into words what everyone else is thinking.

'What's that prick doing with his sticks? He's going to cause an accident.'

Climbing an exposed section of the North Col Wall

Luckily all is OK, and we reach the short traverse before the ladder. The Americans ahead of me are walking very slowly now, stopping every few metres, and I wonder how long it's going to take them to get up the ladder.

But another problem emerges when we reach its foot. At the top, a large group of fifteen Indians and their Sherpas are about to come down, and they couldn't have chosen a worse moment with most of the queuing climbers still arriving beneath the ladder. The Sherpas are very quick, but many of the Indians descend nervously. It's past three o'clock now. The sun disappears behind the seracs above us. We have to wait about half an hour, getting colder and colder while other climbers join the queue behind us, including Grant, Mark and Ian. Luckily when it's our turn to ascend everything goes smoothly, and the people ahead of us are relatively quick going up.

It's four o'clock when we arrive at the North Col campsite at 7,075m, and the sun is no longer warming the tents. We have a great consolation prize though. All our Sherpas have come up today as well, and Grant and I find ourselves sharing a tent with Chongba. While we lie down and rest, he rehydrates us with mint tea and tries to feed us up with what little food we can eat at this altitude, such as soup and noodles.

It's very cramped with three of us, and I have a cold night squeezed up against one wall of the tent with no elbow room. As the night progresses the inside of the tent wall becomes encrusted with ice formed by condensation from our breath, and it's quite uncomfortable as I periodically roll over and rub my head against it. There are going to be few comforts on this summit push.

DAY 37
CLIMBING THE NORTH RIDGE OF EVEREST

Thursday 17th of May, 2012 – Camp 2, Everest, Tibet

It's a beautiful morning, with the sun on the tents early. Chongba boils up water for tea, but I don't feel like breakfast. When Grant asks for soup I feel a little queasy, and when he manages to squeeze down some chicken noodles as well, I struggle not to retch.

It's going to be another long day today, with more than 700m of vertical ascent up the North Ridge to Camp 2. Chongba prepares my oxygen bottle and mask before we depart, and I lay it across the top of my pack, ready to start breathing it halfway up today's snow slope. The plan is to start taking supplementary oxygen at the rate of two litres per minute somewhere between 7,200 and 7,300m, but we'll see how far I get without it. Once we begin using it then we intend to keep doing so until we are back at Camp 1 on the way down. Even at night we'll be sleeping on half a litre per minute.

I leave camp at 7.50, behind most of our team. Within a few minutes of leaving I'm greeted by one of the most amazing views, so jam-packed with peaks that it's difficult to tell them all apart. From Camp 1 itself our view was mainly to the north, down the North Col Wall to the top end of the East Rongbuk Glacier, Advanced Base Camp and the smaller peaks behind, including the innocuous-looking triangles of Khartaphu and Lhakpa Ri. While the slopes of Changtse were up to our left, a

111

high wall of seracs behind camp obscured the view to the south.

Shortly after leaving camp, and before I've started climbing up the North Ridge, I emerge from underneath the seracs and find myself standing on the North Col proper. To my right all the peaks of the Khumbu region of Nepal stretch out before me like a tumble of discarded toys. Most prominent among them is Pumori, a frightening cylindrical peak about level with us at 7,075m. I've been reading the account of the 1922 expedition on my Kindle during our many hours at Base Camp. Mallory gushed about this view in a way I couldn't possibly recreate, even if I were to suck on eight litres of oxygen a minute:

We had now an uninterrupted view of all that lies to the west. Below us was the head of the main Rongbuk Glacier. On the skyline to the left was the prodigious northwest ridge of Everest, flanked with snow, hiding the crest of the West Peak. Past the foot of the northwest ridge we looked down the immense glacier flow south-westwards into Nepal and saw without distinguishing them the distant ranges beyond. Near at hand a sharp edge of rocks, the buttress of Changtse falling abruptly to the Rongbuk Glacier, blocked out vision of the two greatest mountains northwest of Everest, Gyachung Kang and Cho Oyu.

But we could feel no regret for this loss, so enchanted were we by the spectacle of Pumori; though its summit was little higher than our own level, it was, as it always is, a singularly impressive sight. The snow-cap of Pumori is supported by splendid architecture; the pyramidal bulk of the mountain, the steep fall of the ridges and faces to south and west, and the precipices of rock and ice towards east and north, are set off by a whole chain of mountains extending west-north-west along a frail, fantastic ridge unrivalled anywhere in this district for the elegant beauty of its cornices and towers.

No more striking change of scenery could be imagined than this from all we saw to the east, the gentle snowy basin; the unemphatic lines of the slopes below and on either side of the Lhakpa La, dominated as they are by the dullest of mountains, Khartaphu; the even fall of rocks and snow from the east ridge of Changtse and from the northeast ridge of Everest. Pumori itself stood only as a symbol of this new wonderful world before our eyes as we stayed to look westwards, a world exciting, strange, unearthly, fantastic as the skyscrapers in New York City, and at the same time possessing the dignity of what is enduring and immense, for no end was visible or even conceivable to this kingdom of adventure.

George Mallory in The Assault on Everest (ed. Charles Bruce)

He explains it in a lot more detail than I possibly could at this moment in time, but I disagree with him in one respect – or perhaps the serac wall I've emerged from was longer ninety years ago. Behind and to the right of Pumori are two much larger peaks, the higher of which has a flat top from this angle. These can only be Cho Oyu and Gyachung Kang, the two peaks Mallory said he couldn't see.

The greater view, though, is straight ahead of me up the North Ridge. A smooth snow slope rises 400 to 500m, with dozens of figures crawling up it on a fixed rope. It looks almost sheer from where I stand, but slopes always seem deceptively steep when you're looking at them head-on. Above the smooth slope the mountain is mostly rock with a few dapples of snow. Immediately above the snowline the North Ridge continues as a sprawling 400m campsite, Camp 2. This stretches up towards the North-East Shoulder, a place where the North Ridge meets the North-East Ridge, which continues onward to our right, crowning the North Face all the way to the summit. Some people have chosen to camp just above the snowline, but I know our camp is somewhere near the top in order to give ourselves a shorter day tomorrow.

The black rock of Everest's summit ridge and pyramid is a daunting sight, but also inspiring, for the summit is only 1,800m above me, and for the first time it seems within my grasp.

Climbers on the North Ridge, with the summit up above

I plod slowly uphill. To begin with it's not very steep, but the gradient increases the higher I get. I can see what look to be a couple of flatter areas higher up where groups of climbers are sitting down to rest. These areas keep me motivated to push on up an otherwise featureless slope. I'm not the only person needing motivation. Ahead of me I see Mila sit down in the snow.

'I can't carry this big weight,' she says as I pass.

'You can put the juice [oxygen] on if you're tired,' I reply. 'That should get you moving again.'

A little while later I look back and see she's resumed climbing without her oxygen. It's going to be a long old struggle today, and I know there are going to be a few moments like that for me too.

A hundred metres higher I catch up with Mark and Ian in their identical *his and hers* yellow Rab down suits (don't ask me which is which). They are sitting down in the snow and taking a rest. I collapse in a heap next to them.

'How are you feeling?' I ask.

'Fucked,' Mark says. I don't know what I was expecting him to say.

'You're supposed to be. This is Everest,' I reply, still needing to pinch myself that it really is, and the summit's just there above us. 'But you're not thinking of turning round are you?'

'Fuck no!' he grunts.

I don't ask about his fingers. I know from experience that if it's only down to stamina then Mark will struggle on no matter what, but his fingers and toes are the critical factor. He's had to abandon several summits because of frozen digits, including on Manaslu last year when Ian and I both reached the summit. We all want him to succeed, but until any of us actually see him near the summit there will remain that niggling feeling of doubt.

We resume climbing together, with Mark in the lead to begin with. When we reach an anchor point in the fixed ropes at about 7,300m, halfway up the snow slope, we meet Pasang Nima. He's been instructed to wait for each of us in turn, and help us put our oxygen masks on. Although my aim was to reach the snowline before I started on the juice, I don't resist when he reaches inside my pack and fits the mask to my face.

We're noticeably quicker when we set off again, though this feeling only lasts for a short while before the tedious reality of the snow plod takes over again. Ian goes on ahead while Mark and I run into a bottleneck of climbers who walk very slowly, taking only a few steps at a time before stopping to rest – only short pauses, but I find them agonising and would much prefer to continue onwards. They remind me of the weight on my back, and I have to lean forwards on my ice axe with my torso in a horizontal position to pretend the weight isn't there.

After what seems like hours we reach the top of the snow slope, where Ian is waiting with a few other people at the start of the rocks. We plod agonisingly up to join him. Above this the route continues on loose rock. Phil had described this part as a trail, but there's also a fair amount of scrambling required to get up it and I find the more varied terrain easier. It's not long before we pass the first tents, but I know we still have a long way to go before we reach ours.

Camp 2 is a sprawling mass of jagged rock with tents crammed onto every tiny platform. The trail zigzags through, marked by a pink fixed rope to clip into. Most people seem to be camping in the lower sections, and many have just arrived, dumping their kit across the trail and providing additional obstacles to step around.

Higher up there's a lot more space, and tents are no longer crammed onto every shelf. Although it's hard work now I'm glad we've decided to camp right at the top. Eventually I see Chongba above me and give him a wave. I look back and see Ian, Mark and Mila not far behind; it's only three o'clock and our Camp 2 is at 7,815m. I feel like I've made good time, but as I crawl into our tent Grant tells me he's already been here two hours. He ate well at Camp 1 but that's an amazing performance, and he seems to be peaking at just the right time.

Ours is the highest tent in camp, and it feels like we have the luxury villa looking out over the rest of the village. The North Col is out of sight beneath us, and beyond it the summit of Changtse is below us now. There's even some privacy and a few flat areas to go for a reasonably comfortable crap. I take advantage of this opportunity for the last time in three days.

At Chongba's suggestion we devise a new sleeping system, lying crossways inside the tent with the doors to either side. The tent tapers at the doorways, so as the tallest person I have to sleep in the middle, but I try out my new position and discover that it's long enough, and we now have much more space between us.

Grant continues to eat well, wolfing down a packet of dehydrated rice and chicken. Chongba urges me to eat as much as I can, but I struggle. He knows I need the energy – and as my personal Sherpa on summit day, he's keen for me to be successful. He wants to reach the summit too, after all. I force down half a dozen mouthfuls, but then I feel like I'm going to throw up. I take a few deep breaths and manage to keep it down, but that's as much as I can do and I certainly can't eat any more. I snack on fun-sized Snickers and Mars bars, but even they're a struggle. Chongba boils up plenty of tea and juice though, and I feel reasonably well hydrated when we turn into our bags at around seven o'clock.

DAY 38
THE HIGHEST CAMPSITE IN THE WORLD

Friday 18th of May, 2012 – Camp 3, Everest, Tibet

I sleep restlessly, but in the morning Grant tells me he's slept like a baby with his oxygen mask on.

'Lucky you,' I reply. 'The mask's uncomfortable to sleep with. I don't feel I got any benefit from my oxygen.'

He leans over and looks at the regulator on my oxygen cylinder. 'I can see why.'

I look myself, and it's showing the same reading as it did last night, which means I slept with the thing strapped to my face, but didn't actually breathe in any oxygen. I had trouble with the mask on Manaslu last year, and it seems I still haven't quite got the hang of it.

Chongba is in no hurry to depart this morning, and rests in the tent long after the sun has hit without rolling over to put the stove on.

'How far today, Chongba?' Grant eventually asks.

'Today short day. Two hour.'

'Two hours?' we both cry simultaneously. 'For Inji [westerner] or Sherpa?'

'For Inji,' he replies.

I find it hard to believe, as we have four or five hundred metres of vertical ascent today. He is a wise man and I trust him, and if it's true then we really have no reason to hurry this morning only to spend the rest of the afternoon at an inhospitable campsite over 8,000m.

But one by one the rest of our team pass by our tent on their way up; first Ian and Mark at eight o'clock, and then Phil, who stops to tell us it will take five hours. Chongba laughs at this, but it seems more reasonable for me given my usual speed of ascent. I begin to get anxious trapped between my two faster tent mates, and sensing my restlessness Chongba begins hurriedly packing away. He fits my mask to a fresh cylinder, and outside the tent he helps me fit my crampons to my boots, which I had been fumbling with in my hurry to get moving.

Ascending above Camp 2

Grant and I leave Camp 2 at nine o'clock. In one respect Chongba turns out to be right: Grant continues to climb like a maniac and reaches Camp 3 in only two hours, but I take a more laboured pace. The path out of Camp 2 diverts away from the North Ridge and makes a shortcut to the adjoining summit ridge by crossing slabs underneath.

To begin with there's a relatively easy snow-clad trail slanting diagonally upwards. Although I'm much slower than Grant, this type of terrain is no problem for me and I make my own good time up it, overtaking both Mila and Margaret when they stop for a rest. It becomes harder soon afterwards, though. There's a steep snow slope to climb, followed by a short section of rock scrambling. A continuous line of Sherpas seems to be catching me up at this section, and although I wait to let some of them by, there doesn't seem to be any way to make progress other than by climbing in amongst them, and it's exhausting trying to maintain a pace which doesn't slow them down too much. Much of the time I find myself inelegantly hauling myself up the fixed rope with my jumar rather than taking the trouble to climb properly, which would take much longer.

When I reach the top of the scramble I flop down exhausted and find myself sitting next to Chongba and Kami, a younger Sherpa Phil has nicknamed Mad Dog on account of his manic grin. Both are smiling; Chongba asks if I'm OK. I nod as I get my breath back, and I continue to rest for a few minutes after they've gone.

There remains one final agonising snow slope into camp. The trail is no longer slanting up the mountainside; now it turns left to take the direct route upwards. As if to remind me where I am, a howling blizzard wells up and the climbing becomes thoroughly unpleasant as I feel the cold snowflakes whip against my cheeks. At the top I catch up with Mark, and we're surprised to see the first tents of Camp 3 appear out of the gloom. We're on a twenty to thirty-degree slope of loose rock and slabs, in a thick mist with snow lashing against us. I'm exhausted and have no idea where our tents are pitched, but if this campsite sprawls as much as Camp 2 then it's going to take a long time to find them. I consider taking off my pack to get out my radio and call Phil, but behind me I hear Mark shout.

'Look, there's Ian.'

Much to my relief they're only a few metres away from us, but once I'm unclipped from the fixed rope it's not easy making my way across the loose sloping rubble to our tent. Chongba helps me with my crampons again and I climb inside.

This is by far our least comfortable pitch. Our legs are sloping downwards at a considerable angle and I have a large rock right underneath both shoulder blades. As soon as I lie on it I slide down to the bottom of the tent. Grant helps me inflate my Thermarest and suggests I put my boots underneath it to raise the level of the lower part of my body. This makes for an even more irregular surface to lie on, but it works, and keeps me in place without sliding downwards. It's not exactly comfortable though; I'm lying on a bed of rocks.

I spend the afternoon in a state of nervous tension. Eating and drinking proceeds in the same manner as previous days: despite being at 8,210m, the highest campsite in the world and the highest I've ever been in my life, Grant continues to eat like Mr Creosote while I force down what I can. But Chongba keeps us all hydrated as we drink huge quantities of mint tea.

I have a bit of kit adjustment to do in the afternoon – I must find a way to prop the oxygen cylinder vertically inside my otherwise empty pack. This may sound trivial, but in fact it's quite important. During summit day on Manaslu last year the cylinder fell horizontally into the bottom of my pack, which meant the tube on my mask was barely long enough to reach my face and the pack hung at an awkward sideways angle. I must have been hunching my shoulders on the way up in order to keep the mask in place, but I didn't notice until I started to descend. By then my neck and shoulders were so painful that my two-day descent was agonising, and by the time I reached Base Camp I was stooping like a 100-year-old man. It was several days before my neck felt better again, and I'm keen to avoid the problem this time around. Luckily I discover a sleeve for a hydration system in the interior of my pack, which the oxygen cylinder slides into perfectly. I show Chongba so that he knows where to put the cylinder if he ends up changing it for me during our ascent.

Our setting here at Camp 3 is hard to ignore. We are high above the clouds near the top of Everest's sheer North Face, and the rest of the world is far beneath us. It's tempting to laze inside our tent, but Grant and I both summon up the energy to step outside and take photographs of the North-East Ridge and summit pyramid a short distance above us. It doesn't seem very far at all now, but heaven only knows what tomorrow is going to be like. Surprisingly, there's rock all around us, without much evidence of snow apart from a few small patches

We have a series of radio calls between tents as we prepare for our summit attempt. The first is at three o'clock, when Phil gives the final weather forecast that has come through on his satellite phone. The wind speeds are going to be the same as they have been on previous days – very light. It's a good summit window, as predicted during our emergency meeting down at Base Camp. That seems an eternity ago now, and took place in a different world.

We still don't know what time we'll be leaving for the summit. Phil wants to start at 10pm (or 12.15am China time). Athough there are not too many people here at Camp 3, he wants to avoid any potential crowds. The rope fixers of the China Tibet Mountaineering Association are also here, and they want to regulate departure times to avoid traffic jams. Phil says they will schedule us into time slots.

We have a second radio call later in the afternoon, and he says we've been given the 11.30 slot – 1.45am China time. He seems happy enough with this.

With our plans in place, there are three hours left for me to lie back on my rock and boots and try to grab what sleep I can. Very little, as it turns out. Not only is my bed uncomfortable, but there is a very noisy and restless group camped right next to us who keep gibbering on for hours. They eventually leave at ten o'clock and I drift off for a few short minutes, but at 10.30 it's time for us to begin preparing for our summit attempt.

DAY 39
THE FIRST STEP

Saturday 19ᵗʰ of May, 2012, part 1 – Summit Day, Everest,
Tibet

It's 11.30pm Nepali time when we leave and begin walking up
the diagonal trail out of Camp 3. Somewhere high above us this
trail leads up onto the summit ridge at a place called the Exit
Cracks.

I have a problem with my oxygen mask almost immediately.
Every few metres it gags against my nose and mouth, causing
me to suffocate. I loosen it with my hand and allow some
ambient air in, but it's happening too frequently. If I suddenly
start suffocating during a difficult move then it could potentially
be very dangerous. I need to do something about it, so I stop and
remove the mask completely, putting it back on in a different
position.

I've never been very happy with my oxygen apparatus, either
here on Everest or on Manaslu, the only other occasion I've used
it. It seems to be one of the most unreliable pieces of equipment
I've ever used, but it's a very important one. When it works it's
obvious that it's working very effectively, but more often than
not I suspect I'm not getting as much benefit as I should be –
clearly the case in our tent down at Camp 2. The gagging issue
seems to be random. I've repositioned the mask, but I'm going to
have to keep my fingers crossed it doesn't happen again.

Chongba has been waiting patiently while I faff around with

my mask. We move on and I walk slowly for about twenty paces. I breathe a sigh of relief – the gagging problem doesn't re-occur.

A short distance above camp the route becomes a little more technical, with short rocky sections to negotiate. Some of these just involve a few tall steps to climb up, while others are a little harder and I need to use my hands. In most cases I do this by hauling myself up the fixed rope with my jumar.

Time is difficult to gauge: it may be one hour or it may be two, but eventually we reach a significant series of rock scrambles which are tiring to surmount. We all know there are three main technical rock sections on Everest's northern route: the First Step, the Second Step and the Third Step. The climbing that we're having to do is significant enough that I begin to wonder whether we've reached the First Step already. At the top I flop down in a bed of snow. There's a short snow ramp above this, and suddenly nothing beyond: we're on the summit ridge.

For the next few minutes the going is a little easier. The first section of the ridge is at a very gentle gradient, and for a while we walk along it on an easy snow trail. Then the snow peters out and we drop a little to the right of the ridgeline. It's rocky underfoot with a light dusting of snow, and the terrain beneath our feet slopes gently downwards to our right. Up ahead a dozen head torches clearly illuminate one of Everest's main steps. It seems we were the last team to leave camp tonight, and much of the route ahead of us is lit up like lights along a promenade.

I'm keen to know which step we're arriving at. The lights climb almost straight up for a bit then angle across to the right. If this is the Second Step then one of these sections will have a ladder. If there's no ladder then I'll know we've only arrived at the First Step. We've been able to climb without impediment until now, and this is the first bottleneck we've come across on an otherwise quiet summit night. At the bottom of the step is a deep bed of snow a few feet in height. It's easy to climb by planting my feet in previous climbers' footsteps. Bare rock extends above this, and I look up to see there's no ladder; this must be the First Step and the earlier scramble was probably only the Exit Cracks.

It takes us a long time to get up this obstacle as we wait for the climbers ahead of us. I find the climbing easiest by lifting my leg as high as I can onto the boulder above me, then hauling myself up the rope with my jumar. Each boulder is just about big enough to stand on with both feet as I wait for the people above to make their next move. It's tiring work, and at the top of the first vertical section one of them stops for a substantial rest before tackling the second diagonal traverse.

I suppose it's safer for them to be well rested, but Chongba and I are perched on precarious boulders below them and we'd like to be able to get moving. When they eventually climb on we follow directly behind them without resting. The second section is easy scrambling by sea-level standards, but again I rely on the fixed ropes a lot. Because this section is partly a sideways traverse it's going to be a lot more difficult to down-climb. We've climbed up in the dark, and on the way back I'll have the full 2,500m of the North Face to stare down. I'm not looking forward to coming back this way, but I'll have to cross that bridge later.

I'm exhausted when I reach the top, and I have to stop for a long rest to get my breath back. I very nearly vomit into my mask, but manage to check myself. Chongba waits, perhaps wondering whether I'm going to move on from this, but eventually I rise slowly and continue onwards.

DAY 39
THE SECOND STEP

Saturday 19th of May, 2012, part 2 – Summit Day, Everest,
Tibet

The next section between the First and Second Steps is one of the most frightening parts of summit day for me, as I become accustomed to the terror of it all. It's the moment when I first think, 'what the hell am I doing here?' It's when I realise that I'm several levels out of my comfort zone and I become aware that Everest's North-East Ridge is not at all what I was expecting – that it's a rock scramble rather than a snow climb.

It's when I see my first dead body, a Scottish climber who has fallen onto his back with his head pointing down the mountain. It must be about 4.30am Nepali time, for between the First and Second Steps night turns to day. I learn exactly what it is I'm climbing and become aware of the god-forsaken drop to my right.

The 'trail' between the First and Second Steps is a series of very narrow rock ledges just about wide enough for a boot, some horizontal, some sloping downwards at an angle of about thirty degrees. Some hold a light dusting of snow, not much help when you're wearing crampons, but most are bare rock. Quite a few of them contain three or four strands of old fixed rope from previous years for me to snag my crampon points on.

We keep just below the ridgeline, so manage to escape the terror of looking down the Kangshung Face to our left, but to the right of these precarious sloping slabs is a horrifying 2,500m drop down the North Face. As the sun rises, and I become more aware of where I am, I get increasingly nervous. Doubts start creeping in and for the first time a very important mantra comes to my mind: 'whatever happens, I've got to get back down safely'.

Crossing slabs between the First and Second Steps, with the North Face falling to the left

It's almost a relief to reach the foot of the Second Step. By now I've been creeping so nervously across these slabs that any bottleneck there might have been ahead of me has cleared. The climbers who held us up on the First Step have been much quicker through this section, as have my two old pals Mark and Ian whom I see behind, catching me up with their Sherpas Ang Gelu and Kami.

The first part of the Second Step involves a very short ladder into a small alcove. Above this, and to the right of the alcove, is a large diagonally sloping boulder with a crack down the left side broad enough for a boot. Several ropes, old and new, run down the crack in a tangle of nylon. The boulder is several feet high with very few cracks for crampons. Somehow I've got to get my right leg on top of it then haul myself onto the boulder using the ropes. On the other side of the boulder, of course, is a sickening 2,500m drop straight down the North Face, which doesn't exactly spur me on.

I try twice in vain, and my nerves are shredded. 'What the hell am I doing here?' I think to myself again.

By now Chongba has joined me in the alcove. 'I don't think I can do it, Chongba. I'm sorry!'

He looks very sad, but before we can think about our predicament Ang Gelu joins us in the alcove and doesn't hesitate. Mark is waiting to climb the ladder behind him, and I see that turning around is not an option.

'OK. I climb up to the rock and pull you up,' Ang Gelu says.

He is true to his word. I watch him effortlessly perform the manoeuvre I tried in vain. Then he reaches down and proffers a hand, and within moments I have joined him on the rock. The die is cast, and Chongba and I move on past him.

There's a short step onto another rock which slopes back to the left, then an easy snow ramp leads about ten metres up to the Second Step's most famous feature: a tall ladder up a vertical section, left by a Chinese team in 1975. Without this ladder hundreds of lesser climbers like me would never have been able to climb Everest from the north side.

Unlike big smooth rocks, I don't have any problem with ladders, and sure enough within moments I'm up it too. After another six feet of scrambling through a tangle of old ropes, I have overcome the Second Step.

DAY 39
THE THIRD STEP

Saturday 19th of May, 2012, part 3 – Summit Day, Everest, Tibet

At last we're on a slightly broader ridge, and for the first time in a long while I'm able to proceed without having to concentrate on every step. A long walk up a wide snow trail leads to a small rock promontory: the Third Step. Above this the mountain steepens up the final summit pyramid. We see climbers crawling up this steep snow slope, but rocks guard the area above it, so the climbers are angling to the right where there must be a gap in the rocks allowing access to the summit.

Our goal is in sight now, but in reality we still have another four or five hours of climbing before we reach the summit. As we walk up the snow trail I begin to tire and have to stop for a rest. Chongba takes the opportunity of a safe area in which to sit down to change my oxygen bottle for the spare one he's been carrying in his pack. This leads me to believe he thinks we're now halfway through our summit day.

We continue up the broad trail to the Third Step, but I have to stop at the bottom for yet another rest. Tired, with deadened senses, I flop down beside another corpse curled up in a foetal position at the foot of the step. Mark and Ian overtake me with Ang Gelu and Kami; I get up, very tired, and climb the step behind them. It's the easiest of the three steps, but it still involves plenty of hauling myself up with my arms, and my energy is draining rapidly now. There are some horizontal rocks to weave through before reaching the snow slope up the summit pyramid.

Once again I need a rest before I can continue, and I watch Mark and Ian pull away from us up the slope. As I wait I see Chongba reach into my pack and make an adjustment to my oxygen regulator. He tries to do it surreptitiously, and I pretend not to notice.

The mantra comes to mind again: 'must get down safely'. I briefly consider asking Chongba how much further there is to the summit and whether we should consider turning around, but in the end I remain silent. Two main factors motivate me to keep going: my two friends Mark and Ian are up ahead, and I would be gutted if they make it to the summit and I don't. Secondly there is Chongba himself. Although he has climbed Everest twelve times, he's never done it from the north side and I know he's desperate to. Along with all our Sherpas, he's put so much effort into the expedition, carrying superhuman loads up the mountain to ensure all our camps are established. We're nearly there, and while getting back safely is the most important thing, I really don't want to let him down.

As long as he is here and prepared to continue, I'll keep going.

DAY 39
THE SUMMIT PYRAMID

Saturday 19th of May, 2012, part 4 – Summit Day, Everest, Tibet

We move on up the snow slope. Now there are climbers coming down from the summit. I'm too exhausted to climb past them, so I stop on the rope to let each of them pass. Some, like the Sherpas, do this easily, even unclipping from the rope to skip past me and reattach behind; others do it more nervously, grabbing hold of my pack to reach around and reattach their carabiner.

At the top of the snow slope I reach the rock band which guards the summit. The trail edges to the right across a narrow rock ledge. The ledge continues for some distance, and I have no choice but to stare down the abyss. It's not a great place to pass other climbers, but there are now quite a few of them coming down from the summit.

I recognise Phil, Grant and Pasang Nima, but I'm too tired to congratulate them, so I press against the rock face and make myself as small as possible to let them past. Phil is in a talkative mood, though. He notices the air-intake valve on my oxygen mask is iced up, so he blows on it to defrost the ice particles. This is a somewhat intimate procedure, but I'm in no position to worry about whether any passers-by think we're tongue-kissing. The front of my mask has two inlet channels. The first is a tube pulling pure oxygen from the cylinder in my pack – but the human body also needs all the other gases that are found in air, such as nitrogen, so there's another valve on the mask that lets in ambient air from the outside. It's this valve that was iced over, inhibiting my breathing slightly.

'Not far now, dude,' Phil says. 'Everyone's done amazing. Grant summited. Mila summited. Mark Dickson summited. Ian Cartwright summited. It's just five minutes to the top from here.'

It's a morale-boosting statement, and it certainly encourages me to continue. Unfortunately the last part is also complete bullshit. Five minutes, my arse. Phil only said it to make me feel better and ensure I don't think about turning back. There is still another hour at my exhausted pace.

There's a real flurry of people on their way down now. As I edge further round the ledge my hat gets caught in the wind and goes flying down the North Face into Tibet, but I don't care: if I get to the top and back down again it's a worthwhile sacrifice. Halfway along the traverse I have to wait a very long time as climbers edge past me one by one, but ordinary politeness doesn't exist on this narrow ledge on the roof of the world. Nobody stops to give us our turn to proceed.

Eventually there's a gap. We continue to where the ledge ends and the trail turns sharply upwards through a gap in the rock band. I guess you could call this the Fourth Step, a scramble over the rocks guarding the summit. I haul myself up with my jumar. It's tiring work as always, but we still have to keep stopping for long periods to let people past, so I get plenty of opportunity to rest.

I recognise Mila in her red down suit, but I'm not in celebratory mood just yet.

'Congratulations on reaching the summit,' I say, 'but take care, won't you.'

She doesn't look like she needs reminding. Staring down this tricky rock section, we're all too aware there's a long way to go before we're safe again.

Finally Chongba and I reach the snow slopes above the rock band, and the summit feels very close. I turn right and begin plodding slowly up a gentle rise. At the brow I see prayer flags on the horizon a few hundred metres in front of me: the summit, the highest point in the world!

But there's a little way to go yet. The trail weaves gently around a couple of snow humps before rising up to the flags. I can see several figures amongst the tangle of red, yellow, green and blue. Two are in yellow down suits, and I believe they might be Mark and Ian, but as I get nearer I see Mark and Ang Gelu are sitting in a sheltered spot beneath one of the snow humps. Ian and Kami are the two on the summit; they begin descending and reach Mark and Ang Gelu before us. I shake hands with my two old friends as I pass them, but I don't stop for a chat with the top so close. This is a long, drawn-out advance to the summit, and I'm keen to get it over with as soon as possible.

Although our approach was quite sheltered, the prayer flags on the summit are billowing wildly, so I know it must be windy up there. I mount the final snow steps with my eye on a spot to sit down, but just as I get there someone else takes it with a whoop. I look over his shoulder and find myself staring down the South-East Ridge. It's crawling with people coming up from the south side in Nepal. The man who took my seat has just arrived from that direction himself.

It doesn't matter. I turn around and give Chongba a big hug. This is his thirteenth time up here and he seems happy, but for me there's no sense of elation or achievement. Relief perhaps, yes, but I know how far we still have to go, and the descent is going to be very difficult.

I take a few photographs and ask Chongba to take some of me. It's ten o'clock Nepali time exactly, and not as cold as I was expecting. I've been wearing only my inner gloves since the Third Step. Usually my camera batteries need warming up before taking the summit pictures, but here they just work. I dimly realise we've been very lucky with the weather – it's been a perfect summit day until now.

It's busy up here, though, and the wind isn't tempting me to stick around. The descent looms large in my mind; I know there's still a long ordeal ahead of us. We start descending after only about five minutes on the summit. Whether I will ever be here again on the top of the world doesn't cross my mind. My only focus now is to get down safely.

Mark on the summit of Everest (8848m), the highest point on Earth, with Makalu behind

DAY 39
THE WORLD'S HIGHEST GRAVEYARD

Saturday 19ᵗʰ of May, 2012, part 5 – Summit Day, Everest, Tibet

We stop and rest for a few minutes in the sheltered spot below the summit where I saw Mark and Ian. It's quiet here away from the wind, providing an opportunity to compose my thoughts. All the crowds that passed us as we ascended the rock band have evaporated. Chongba and I seem to be the very last people on the summit from the north side, and now we're completely alone. The peace and solitude up here would be sensational but for the need to descend. I begin repeating the mantra to myself again: 'must get down safely, must get down safely'.

I get into difficulty almost immediately when we resume our descent. I stumble as we're scrambling through the rock band and have to sit down. Two pieces of equipment have been making my progress difficult and I need to stop and fix them.

My goggles have been steaming up regularly and inhibiting my vision, so every few minutes I'm having to stop and clean them. My vision becomes completely blurred at the most inconvenient moments. I have to wear them or I will become snowblind, but I need a more permanent solution or our descent is going to take for ever. Chongba takes out his pocket knife and makes a few emergency adjustments to improve the ventilation.

Meanwhile I take a look at my second problem item: my oxygen mask, which keeps getting pulled away from my face.

The oxygen cylinder is supposed to sit inside a narrow sleeve inside my pack to prevent it falling over and taking the tube attached to my mask with it. When I look inside my pack, I see that when Chongba changed the bottle below the Third Step, he didn't put the new one back inside the sleeve – now it's just lying at an awkward angle at the bottom of my pack. This means the pack rests at an uncomfortable angle across my shoulders, but more importantly the tube isn't long enough to reach my face, which explains why the mask keeps getting pulled off. I'm angry with myself for allowing Chongba to change the bottle without checking to see he'd put it back in the sleeve. I had serious problems with this on Manaslu last year, and I knew how important it was to ensure it didn't happen again.

While I'm putting the bottle back into the sleeve, I notice the flow rate on the regulator has been turned down to one litre a minute. Chongba must have done this when I saw him reach for the regulator while we were resting at the top of the Third Step. He was probably worried about me running out of oxygen during our descent. We have sixteen hours of oxygen at two litres a minute, but if we take any longer than this there would be a danger of me running out before we reach the safety of Camp 3. Although I'll be even slower at just one litre a minute, at least there is no longer a risk of the cylinder running out.

With the adjustments done we're ready to continue our descent, but I wonder what thoughts must be going through Chongba's head. On his own he would be down the mountain in no time, but waiting for me must be very irritating, not to mention worrying. Here we are with almost the entire descent ahead of us, and already I'm looking shaky.

'Sorry, Chongba,' I say. 'I know I'm tired, and I want to descend very carefully.'

Luckily this is only a minor hiccup. We descend through the rest of the rock band and traverse the rock ledges without a hitch. It helps that we don't meet any more people coming up. As we're approaching the Third Step down the steep snow slope I feel confident enough to take my camera out and take some photographs.

I can see at least three dead bodies at the top of the Third Step, and I know that a fourth lies curled up at the bottom. As you're climbing, the Third Step's position at the foot of the summit pyramid makes it look deceptively close to the top – but there are still many hours to go. This might explain why so many people have lost their lives here, making that final effort to reach their goal, though it also suggests they may have forgotten that getting down safely is just as important. Today's goal for me is Camp 3, and the summit was just a point on the way.

You might think these corpses motivate the descending climber to keep going, but I don't think they have that effect at all. As I approach the top of the Third Step one of the bodies is directly level with my eye line to the left of the trail. Its final resting place is in an unusual position halfway up a short rock face on the north side of the step, which makes it look like it's trying to scramble back up the rocks and crawl onto the trail ahead of me, like some sort of high-altitude zombie. It's very disturbing, and there's no way I can ignore it till I've got past.

The Third Step itself proves easier to down-climb than I thought it would be. There are just two steep drops, which I'm able to overcome by sitting on the edge, dangling my legs over and carefully lowering myself onto the rock below.

At the bottom of the step I meet another climber waiting to come up. I don't pay much attention to them, and can't even be sure if they're male or female, but the significance only occurs to me later. Not only are they alone, but there's nobody else behind and it will still be many hours before they reach the summit. It's much too late to be continuing up – if they keep on going it's very likely they'll be descending in the dark. They should be turning around now. I'm so absorbed in my own struggle for survival that it doesn't occur to me to get involved in the affairs of others. I say nothing to them and we continue onwards.

DAY 39
DICING WITH DEATH

Saturday 19ᵗʰ of May, 2012, part 6 – Summit Day, Everest, Tibet

It doesn't take us long to descend the broad snow ridge to the top of the Second Step. As we approach we can still see a number of climbers on the ridge beyond, including the distinctive matching yellow down suits of Mark and Ian.

I descend the first six-foot section of the Second Step by grabbing a handful of half a dozen old ropes and lowering myself onto a platform just to the left of the top of the ladder. I figure I only need one of the ropes to hold firm and I'll be safe enough, and so it proves. I clip into the pink rope alongside the ladder, which I hope is the new one, and carefully climb down to the snow ramp.

Here I have to wait for a young European climber wearing big red boots with a Crispi logo down the side, who in turn appears to be waiting for a Sherpa ahead to give him the all clear. It's the first of several long waits on the Second Step that end up delaying us half an hour to an hour.

I can see the climber is very nervous, and it's unclear how much help the Sherpa is providing, or whether it's even his own Sherpa.

Time passes, I have no idea how slowly. I wait for at least ten minutes at the top of the snow ramp. Then, when I'm able to move on, I descend just a few metres before I'm delayed a similar length of time at the bottom of it. Eventually I'm able to proceed across the sloping platform until I'm standing on top of the very rock I had difficulty climbing on our way up. On that occasion Ang Gelu had to give me a helping hand, but it's a different story now.

Chongba waits below the main ladder on the Second Step

I stand atop the rock for what feels like another fifteen minutes while the climber dithers in the alcove below. A single step to my left is the horrifying 2,500m drop down the North Face, and every once in a while I have to edge across my platform and peer round the corner to see if the alcove below me has been vacated.

There was a time when this situation might have terrified me, but now my senses have been deadened and I realise I'm a lot more confident than the climber below me. In fact, my overwhelming emotion is boredom. I wonder what's taking him so long when all he has to do is step down the smaller ladder. I see the Sherpa reach the bottom of the ladder which marks the end of the Second Step and start crossing the slabs beyond. He stumbles briefly but keeps his footing, leaving the other climber alone in the alcove. Perhaps it's not his Sherpa after all?

Eventually the climber moves, and within seconds I've swung down into the alcove in the same manner that I reached the upper ladder, by grabbing half a dozen old ropes and lowering myself down. As soon as he reaches the bottom of the lower ladder I'm on it too, and I climb down to join him.

I'm now at the bottom of the Second Step, but if I think I'm free to move on across the slabs, I'm sadly mistaken. The other climber is standing in my way and won't let me past. His behaviour becomes increasingly erratic.

There are two small ladders here, but the second one appears to be redundant. He begins rattling it – not only can I not get past him, but Chongba, waiting in the alcove, can't come down. It's infuriating. I politely ask what he's doing but he ignores me and continues rattling the ladder. I try to get past by reaching round him and attaching my carabiner to the rope the other side of him, but as soon as I attach it he slips backwards, pulling me fast against him.

He apologises, but now we're both stuck. He won't let me past, or allow Chongba down the ladder. I can feel my frustration boiling inside. It should be straightforward, but he's making such a meal of our situation. I extricate myself from this awkward position by unclipping my carabiner and reattaching it to the rope my side of the climber. This enables me to step out of his way again, but he's still in mine, and he continues to rattle the ladder for a few minutes longer.

Finally, after what seems an eternity, he moves on, but I notice the pink rope is looped around the foot of the main ladder. I start to unloop it so it doesn't cause a problem for Chongba when he comes down, but as soon as I begin to do so the climber screams at me:

'Nooo!'

I realise that he was faffing around with the ladders to make the fixed rope tighter by creating an additional anchor point. I let him move on, as it's better to get him out of the way and let Chongba look after himself. Chongba descends the ladder without difficulty and we inch our way across the slabs behind the other climber. He is taking for ever and keeps stopping every few steps.

'Excuse me, can we get past, please,' I shout during one particularly long wait.

He ignores me and remains stationary.

'Excuse me, please can you get to the next anchor, and then we will overtake.'

Hallelujah! This appears to work. The next anchor is only six feet away. He moves up to it without pausing, and waits to let us clip past him. He's been extremely polite whenever he's spoken to me, but his behaviour has been impossible and has delayed us far more than it needed to. I don't know how far behind the others we are now, but there are more hazards to come.

And the nervous climber isn't finished with us yet. Towards the end of the next slab I feel my feet pulled from underneath me and I struggle to keep my balance.

'What the fuck!' I cry.

I look back and see that he's fallen over onto the slab. In his fall he must have jerked the bits of old rope underneath him, which I also happened to be standing on.

My only thought is that it's a huge relief to be past him. It doesn't occur to me to go back and help, and nor do I consider whether he will make it down safely. It's getting late and I'm locked in my own battle for survival. My safety hangs by the most slender of threads – a thread which isn't strong enough for two people. I believe, I hope, I have enough left in me to get myself down safely, but I can't play hero for anyone else. The possibility doesn't even cross my mind.

Soon this fact is illustrated starkly.

The first few slabs beyond the Second Step are the narrowest and most dangerous. Once past these the next ones are wider. It's often on the safer parts of the climb where you lose concentration, and so it proves now. I put one of my crampons down on a bit of snow which turns out to be a smooth, sloping rock. Before I know what's happened the crampon slides from under me and I fall two metres into a bed of snow. I've managed to dig my axe firmly in, but the fixed rope is taut at my waist, and I'm almost certain this has saved me.

I heave myself wearily out of the snow and climb back onto the path, breathing heavily. Chongba watches impassively above me, and not for the first time I wonder what's going through his mind.

Just beyond where I fell another figure lies blissfully unaware of my troubles. The body of the Scottish climber rests only a few feet away. He must have fallen here too, but our stories are very different. He fell head first and onto his back, while I fell feet first onto my belly. If he were still conscious then he must have been too exhausted to get up; and worst of all for him, there was nobody to help. Chongba didn't try to help me – he has allowed me to solve every little problem in my own way, but he hasn't left my side, and I know as long as breath remains in my body he will stay there. On a long and dangerous descent it's hard to describe how comforting this is.

But my struggle isn't over.

DAY 39
THE LAST RESERVES

Saturday 19th of May, 2012, part 7 – Summit Day, Everest, Tibet

We move on to our next obstacle, the First Step. Ever since we climbed it near the start of a very long day, it's been a worry in the back of my mind. The descending traverse across the rock face at the top of the step, with the full horror of the North Face unavoidably below, has been a big concern. At the summit I pictured it in my mind as the crux of the descent. If we can make it down this one safely then I know all will be well, at least until Camp 3.

I stare nervously down the first diagonal traverse, wondering how on earth I'm going to get down. I glance back up at Chongba and he waits patiently above me, but I know there's nothing he can do to help. It's up to me to find a way down.

Luckily once I've plucked up the courage to begin descending I move confidently enough, carefully lowering myself from step to step while keeping the fixed rope tight behind me with my right hand. This provides stability, and when I cross the last slab at the bottom of the traverse and reach the anchor point I breathe a sigh of relief.

Although the second section is steeper, it's also more direct, which means I'm able to secure myself with my figure-of-eight device and abseil down (the only occasion I abseil on the climb). It may not be the most elegant way of descending, and for a confident climber it isn't really necessary, but in my present state of mental and physical exhaustion it feels the safest. I go for a slight swing on the very last step, and I hear Chongba gasp at the anchor point above me, but I'm safely down.

I've reached the bottom of the First Step, and in my mind I believe I'm going to be safe.

The reality is very different. As we continue along the easy slabs below the First Step I can feel my rucksack swinging at an awkward angle on my back. Despite securing the oxygen bottle after I left the summit, I realise there's still something wrong with the straps and it's wearing me out.

I spy a small alcove to the side of the trail where I can sit down and sort my pack out, but as I approach I realise yet another dead body occupies it. I didn't see this one on the way up because we passed by here in the dark, but now I can see the body clearly with its striking luminous footwear. It's Green Boots, the Indian climber who crawled into what must have seemed like a cosy little cave during his descent in 1996, and has been here ever since. In 2006 a British climber called David Sharp lay down next to him, and forty people controversially walked past as he lay dying. Some stopped to help, but he was too far gone and died soon after. They removed his body from the trail the following year by dropping it over the Kangshung Face, but nobody has dignified Green Boots by doing the same for him.

It doesn't occur to me either, but it's not going to do my shredded nerves any good to sit down next to him, so I continue onwards until he's out of sight.

The rest of the descent is agonising. I must have mentally shot my bolt at the bottom of the First Step, when there was still a great deal of difficult terrain ahead of me. I had forgotten about all the scrambling below the ridge, particularly the Exit Cracks. I groan when I see them. They're a real shock – I have to dig deep for fresh reserves of mental energy to overcome them.

Physically I'm wrecked. I'm so exhausted I can only go for a few metres at a time before stopping for a rest. Chongba has the patience of a saint, and says nothing as he stops behind me and waits. Twice during rest breaks I feel myself drifting off into sleep. These are called microsleeps. They only last for a few seconds and I'm scarcely aware of them, but I realise I need to stay constantly alert, check myself and stay awake. They could so easily turn into a sleep of exhaustion from which I never wake. Although I have Chongba to prod me into action if he becomes concerned, I owe it to both of us to stay alert.

I hear Grant's voice come over the radio in Chongba's pocket.

'I'm anxious about Mark. He's taking so long. He should be back at the tent by now, and I'm getting worried.'

Phil's voice responds. He seems less concerned. I hear Chongba bark something back in Nepali, presumably to tell them we're both safe.

Little by little we see the tents below us getting nearer, but still I have to keep resting. Chongba never complains, and doesn't try to hurry me up. I can't describe how reassuring his presence is.

We reach Camp 3 at 5.30 after eighteen hours of climbing. Grant is lying on one side of the tent and has been there since midday. I begin to understand how lonely he must have felt lying there on his own, waiting more than five hours for me and Chongba to return. If I were him I would have been worried about us too.

I've had no food and only one litre of water since I departed for the summit eighteen hours ago. I can't remember the last time my throat was so dry. I retch into the vestibule, but there's nothing to come out, although a small piece of my gullet appears to be trying. I remember an incident from one of the old Everest expeditions of the 1920s, when one of the climbers, Somervell I think, experienced breathing difficulties on the way down, and coughed so hard he ended up dislodging a frozen bit of his throat and spitting it out. Once dislodged his breathing returned to normal and he was able to continue. My throat feels like that, and I really want to cough up the bit of my gullet that feels like it's hanging loose, but at the same time I realise it might be a bad idea.

We snuggle up next to Grant and try to make ourselves as comfortable as possible. I remember the big rock below my shoulders, and slip my boots alongside it underneath my mat. Chongba is tired too; Grant proves to be a good tent mate by offering to take over the stove duties. He boils up a few mugs of water, but it's very slow at this altitude, and he would need to boil an ocean to relieve my thirst. He even empties my pee bottle for me – a task many tent mates would refuse – although some of my pee is still frozen around the rim, and he ends up burning a bit of the tent fabric trying to melt it with a match. I have about a litre of tea and water, enough to stop my gullet detaching itself, but still my throat is parched.

The summit is the last thing on our minds as we settle in for an uncomfortable night.

DAY 40
THE INDESCRIBABLE FEELING OF BEING ALIVE

Sunday 20th of May, 2012 – Advanced Base Camp (ABC), Everest, Tibet

Despite my exhaustion the previous day, I get very little sleep. Halfway through the night I notice my oxygen has run out, and I have to wake Chongba who finds a spare bottle and helps me to change it. I sleep a little better after this.

By the morning my sleeping bag is covered in snow, and next to me Grant is looking like a snowman. The tent door next to him is partially open and spindrift has blown in throughout the night. It's howling a gale outside, and although I'm still as thirsty as Oliver Reed in a coffee shop there's little point in trying to light the stove.

'Too windy for stove,' Chongba says. 'We go down now.'

He's right. The only sensible thing for us to do in this gale is to pack away as quickly as possible and head down the mountain. It's a depressing thought. It's going to be another long, tough day, but ABC is only 1,800m below us, and that's reassuring to know.

It's painful getting ready. I end up having to use my pee bottle in the middle of the tent with the others packing around me. Peeing in this wind wouldn't be a happy experience and the risk of frostbite doesn't bear thinking about. I've had so little to drink in the last thirty-six hours that my urine is dark brown and looks like real ale – not that I'm tempted to drink it.

Outside the tent other team members have already packed and are leaving one by one. The wind is hammering down the rocky slope of Camp 3, and an old plastic bag and a sleeping mat strike me on their journey down the North Face. I rush to put my crampons on but struggle with them. For the third day in a row Chongba has to help me with this normally routine task. The Sherpas are struggling with lashing tent poles as they work furiously to put the tents away, and it seems certain something else will be lost in the violent wind.

I'm ready to leave just after seven o'clock, and inch my way across the rocky slope to get back onto the trail and clip into the fixed rope. I have a new problem this morning. Fed up with my snow goggles fogging up yesterday, I decide to wear my Julbo sunglasses instead, but these are even worse. Every rope length I have to stop and wipe them clean, only to see them fog up again almost immediately. I can hardly see where I'm going, but there's easily enough sun to cause snowblindness if I don't wear them, so I struggle on, cursing my luck.

None of the route seems familiar from when we came up, but the pink rope leads me onwards in the direction of Camp 2. After about half an hour, in sheer desperation, I decide to try my snow goggles again. Much to my surprise they don't steam up, and I suddenly have perfect vision again. Yesterday the goggles were dreadful and it doesn't make sense – I will never understand how any of this equipment works! It doesn't matter, though. I'm just relieved to be able to see again.

I quickly descend to Camp 2 on a straightforward path overlooking the North Col far below. When I reach the rocky slabs at the top of Camp 2 where our tents used to be, I sit down for a rest and feel satisfied that the first part of my long descent is over. The wind isn't so fierce here, and for the first time since summit day I feel relaxed as I look upon the breathtaking view across Changtse – a view that in all probability I will never see again. At some point today it may begin to sink in, and I will start to understand what we've achieved.

There's still a long way to go, and it takes another three hours to reach the North Col. The first part is laboured as I tread carefully between the rocky outcrops on the zigzagging trail between the tents of Camp 2. Torn fabric and broken tent poles sway in the breeze – the wind has trashed many of the tents. I have to be careful where I'm putting my feet and can't rely upon the safety of the fixed rope, which has already become badly frayed in places from the many jagged rocks that make up the terrain here.

This has to be one of the most sprawling campsites in the world. I have to stop frequently. A Sherpa overtakes and greets me with enthusiasm, but he's wearing an oxygen mask and I can't work out who he is.

'Are you OK?' he says. I can see by his eyes that he's smiling cheerfully as Sherpas always do.

I've been having trouble with my oxygen mask slipping again, and I ask him if he can help me fit it properly. Only when he's finished do I realise he isn't one of our Sherpas at all, but Mingma who works for the Asian Trekking team. Mark and I know him from an expedition in the Annapurnas many years ago, and it's typical of him to help me out with my kit even though he's not working for us. The mask fits perfectly when he's finished, and I feel like I'm getting more benefit from the oxygen when I resume my descent. Before he leaves he even gives me a boiled sweet.

I'm glad when I finally descend through Camp 2 and reach the snowfield. I rush down (well, maybe not *rush* down) the fixed ropes, hand-wrapping past each one in turn. I'm still tired, and I stop and sit down every two or three anchors, but the going is much easier now and it only takes an hour to descend the 500 vertical metres of the snowfield.

As I walk slowly up the rise into the North Col campsite, I wonder what I'm going to find there. I know I'll need a long rest before tackling the steep slopes of the North Col Wall, so I'm pleasantly surprised to find Phil, Mark, Ian, Grant and Mila sitting outside the tents sunning themselves. It's 11.30 when I flop down next to them. The weather is pleasant again – a wonderful contrast to the howling gales of Camp 3.

This hour in the sun at Camp 1 is just what I need. Somebody gets hold of some water, and I begin the long process of rehydrating. The liquid soothes my sandpaper-dry throat, and I can feel the little bit of loose gullet still hanging on.

Not everything about this hour is comforting though. Phil tells me a man died of exhaustion on his way down from the summit yesterday, and I immediately think of the young climber with the big red Crispi boots who held us up on the Second Step. He was slow and ponderous, and appeared to have great difficulty with the rock scrambling on the North-East Ridge. Perhaps he wasn't a competent enough scrambler to be tackling Everest yet, but to think he died after we passed him – it makes me very sad. What he needed most was someone to help him, and persuade him to turn around when they realised he was going too slowly. I know I couldn't have helped him in the state I was in, but still it makes me feel terrible.

Then I remember the man we passed at the bottom of the Third Step, still going up very late in the day. He had many hours to go before he reached the summit, and if he kept on going then he would be putting his life at risk for sure. I could have helped this man – I could have told him how far he still had to climb. It wouldn't have taken much for me to do this, and it might have made a difference.

If somebody died yesterday then it was almost certainly one of those two, and it's very poignant because the death was preventable. All they needed to do was remind themselves of the mantra *must get down safely*, the words that were echoing around in my head for almost the whole of summit day. They needed to be told that getting to the summit really doesn't matter if you can't get down again.

Margaret was one person with a bit more wisdom. I learn that she was the only one of us who didn't summit. She was suffering from an infection, and at the Third Step she realised she was going too slowly. She went no further. She was behind me at the time, so it was a decision that probably saved her life. I'm sorry for her, but she is already an Everest summiteer, so perhaps her disappointment is not so crushing. And her Sherpa was Chedar, who is the only one of them who had already summited from the north side.

After an hour of resting on the North Col I leave with Mila for the final leg of our journey, the last really dangerous bit of the whole climb. In an hour or so, when we touch down on the ice plateau 400m below us, we'll know that we're safe and the relief will be palpable.

But, in an earlier rotation two weeks before, I found the steep ice gully down to the ladder beneath the North Col absolutely terrifying – so much so that I christened it the *Ladder of Death*. After all the scrambling high up on the North-East Ridge yesterday, however, it feels positively tame. The steps are now like huge great buckets. I stroll down them easily and onto the ladder. Still, I'm relieved, and feel a few minutes closer to safety as I sit in the snow at the bottom.

I look out over Khartaphu and Lhakpa Ri on the horizon in front of me, and wait for Mila to follow. She has a little more difficulty with it, but not through fear. As she moves off the gully and onto the ladder, a rope becomes looped around the sleeping mat tied to the back of her rucksack. Each time she walks down a couple of steps, the rope tightens and she can descend no further. I sit at the bottom of the ladder staring out over the ice plateau, giving her as much time as she needs, and I don't see what's happening. She's saved by Phil, who arrives at the top of the gully and calls down to me when he sees she isn't getting anywhere. I can see immediately what the problem is, and shout back up to Phil, who climbs down to her and unloops the rope.

Mila is breathing heavily when she joins me on the bed of snow beneath the ladder. She must have been worried when she realised she couldn't move down the ladder, and although I've had a good long rest and am ready to continue, there's no hurry and I can wait a little longer.

'Sit down, Mila, and get your breath back,' I tell her. 'We have all the time in the world now.'

She sits down in the snow, and Phil speeds on ahead as we wait for her to recover her breath. She doesn't need long. Soon we're moving again, but we take our time and complete the descent at a leisurely pace. After every steep and tiring section we stop for a rest in the snow and get our breath back. I never forget the mantra – *must get down safely* – but each time we stop I know we're a little closer.

It's a massive feeling of relief when we touch down on the ice plateau at the bottom of the wall and trudge wearily across it. The technical parts are over; now it's just one foot in front of the other. When we reach Crampon Point at the bottom of the ice plateau, two of our Tibetan kitchen boys are waiting for us with milk tea and hot orange juice. I don't protest when they reach down and take off our crampons for us as we sit, exhausted, and rehydrate.

I reach ABC at four o'clock in the afternoon after a laboured stagger along the moraine, stopping frequently. I realise the back of my down suit must have been badly torn yesterday as I scrambled down rocks on the North-East Ridge. I leak feathers from my backside as I walk, and they fly past me in the breeze.

It hasn't sunk in yet; I still can't comprehend what I've achieved, but it's just a five-hour walk back to Base Camp now. I have a tent to myself here at ABC, and the dining tent is a few short paces away. I can begin to eat and drink again after five days on the mountain.

The feeling of relief is hard to express in words; it's like no feeling I've ever experienced before. I know I brushed with death up there. It's the closest I've ever come while being aware of it. Maybe it sounds melodramatic to say this, but I feel like a prisoner who's been granted another chance – a chance to live that I certainly won't take for granted. The feeling is indescribable, but very satisfying. I'm safe again.

DAY 41
HEAVENLY REST

Monday 21ˢᵗ of May, 2012 – Advanced Base Camp (ABC),
Everest, Tibet

We have the blissful experience of enjoying a rest day here at ABC before we continue to Base Camp tomorrow. After six consecutive days of hard toil and eating very little, it's hugely appreciated.

The kitchen tent is quite empty at breakfast time. Our Sherpas have gone back up to Camp 1 to dismantle the tents. I can't imagine how they're able to do this after the summit push. Most of us are like zombies this morning, apart from Grant, who is unspeakably boisterous. I'm physically and mentally very tired, and my body seems to be compensating by filtering out anything superfluous. This means Grant's jokes go over my head like a raven passing over camp, only much higher, barely registering on my consciousness.

Luckily, Phil is finding himself the butt of most of them, and he's in much better shape than the rest of us. After comparing notes from summit day we realise he blew on most of our masks when he passed each of us on his way down from the summit, allegedly to defrost the ambient air-intake valve. Mark accuses him of 'trying to give his clients a good tonguing'.

On a less frivolous note he also brings news from elsewhere on the mountain. He has learned there were four deaths on the south side during our summit day two days ago, and possibly two on the north side.

I'm shocked. When combined with all the Sherpa deaths earlier in the season on the south side, this would make 2012 one of Everest's deadliest years. Although most of the fatalities occurred on the south side, the two on the north (if confirmed) shock me more, because we had perfect weather and the route really wasn't that crowded. The most likely reason for deaths in these circumstances is bad decision making – people continuing to the summit when they should be turning back.

It's all just rumour at the moment, though, and there's even the possibility some people braved the howling gale yesterday morning to try for the summit. This means the fatalities could have occurred yesterday instead. But if two died on Saturday then I know who they were and I passed them by. I try to summon emotion and compassion for these people. In my exhaustion my feelings are dead, and I find it very hard to comprehend.

It's a day of total rest today. I barely leave my tent for a moment, not even to pee; I use my pee bottle and empty it in the back vestibule. Pemba cooks some delicious chicken dishes, but my stomach is still recovering from five days up high, eating very little, and I can't eat so much yet. On the other hand, my throat is slowly recovering from its sandpaper dryness. I no longer feel like a small piece of my throat is about to be retched out.

The rest day is heaven.

DAY 42
THE LAST OBSTACLE

Tuesday 22nd of May, 2012 – Base Camp, Everest, Tibet

One last wee push, just a few short hours of exercise, and then it's done. But at least we don't have to climb any more; it's just trekking from now on, so what could possibly go wrong?

I made a point of not doing any packing yesterday because I wished to have a day of complete rest. Phil wanted us to have a 6.30 breakfast this morning so we could be down in Base Camp as early as possible, but 6.30 is the moment the sun hits the tents here in ABC, and the moment the temperature inside the tent changes from absolutely bloody freezing to really quite tolerably warm. The idea we should wake up, get dressed and start packing away our sleeping bags during the absolutely bloody freezing phase, especially in our still-exhausted state, when we could wait just a few minutes longer and do it all in comparative comfort, seems unnecessarily silly – especially now we have no need to hurry.

Mark and I said last night that 7.30 was the earliest either of us could be dragged to breakfast. Normally this tactic wouldn't work because Phil would respond with the countermeasure of getting the Sherpas to pack away our tents while we're still inside them, but today the Sherpas are exhausted too. They went back up to the North Col yesterday to retrieve Camp 1 while we rested, so this is the first morning they've had a chance to rest since the start of our summit push. They've earned a lie-in if ever

155

anyone did. Mark and I are safe.

I intended to do some packing before breakfast, but in the end I'm still too tired. When I do rise and head for the kitchen tent for breakfast, all my movements are in slow motion. It's good that we have plenty of time, because I'm going to need it today.

Grant and Phil, the regular early birds and also the least tired of us, threatened to leave before breakfast when we talked about it last night, and Grant actually does leave early. Phil joins us for an omelette but leaves while we're still eating.

It takes me about an hour to complete my packing. I do so in a daze. It's a job I could easily do in twenty minutes when moving at normal speed, as it basically just involves stuffing everything inside my duffle bag. My rucksack is extremely light. All I have inside is a bottle of water and an extra jacket. Most of the weight seems to be taken up by the radio that I've been carting around with me every day because it might just save my life. In the end I never used it.

At nine o'clock I put my duffle bag outside the tent for the kitchen crew to pack away and give to the yakpas, and then I start descending. I'm the last of us to leave. My main priority on the trek down to Base Camp is to avoid yaks. Having carefully scrambled down the Third, Second and First Steps on summit day, and survived the hazards of the *Ladder of Death* and the North Col Wall two days ago, I've nearly managed to come back from Everest alive and in one piece. But having watched a companion get charged by a yak while I was trekking in Bhutan three years ago, I've concluded that being mauled by a yak is the most likely cause of death on the last leg of my journey, the otherwise easy if tedious trek back to Base Camp. It would be a silly, almost comical, way to go having done the really hard bit, and too embarrassing to contemplate.

For three hours everything goes well. I make it down to the icy pinnacles of Changtse Base Camp in little more than an hour, having not seen another soul, and I give myself a short rest. The tedious, windy, ankle-twisting section from Changtse Base Camp to Interim Camp takes a little longer – in fact, it drags on and on if I'm honest – but slowly the scenery changes and I feel like I'm making progress.

It's just short of Interim Camp that I meet the yaks, and it's the worst possible place. The trail drops down steeply off the medial moraine of the Magic Highway to cross a frozen river and climb back up the other side on another steep bank of moraine. Anywhere else and it would have been possible to just step off the path and let the many tons of bovine flesh and sharp horns safely past, but not here – here it's just steep rubble that slides from underneath my boots, and dozens of the blasted animals are heading towards me.

I find a small flat area just above the frozen river and wait. It probably takes about half an hour for them all to come through, and they're quite jumpy because the yakpas keep shouting and hurling rocks at them, but in the end none of them charge me. I then have to trudge back up the moraine bank on the other side of the river, keeping my fingers crossed another confounded herd of them doesn't suddenly appear over a brow. Then I'd be really stuffed. I doubt if I have the energy to hurl myself up a bank of loose rocks to try and evade them, and jumping down would put me right in the firing line of rockfall. Luckily it doesn't happen, and past Interim Camp it's a bit safer, for there are places to step off the path again.

But now I have other hazards to contend with. I meet another climber coming up the other way on the start of his own summit push, looking nearly as tired as I do (at least that's my impression – to him I probably look like I'm at death's door). He quizzes me about my summit push, how many hours it took me, how many bottles of oxygen I used and at what flow rate. I really can't be bothered, but I answer his questions as politely as I can, and try to sound vaguely interested when he starts telling me about his own hopes and intentions. It's a relief when I find an excuse to continue.

It's 3.30 when I arrive back at Base Camp. It's taken me six and a half hours, exactly the same amount of time it took me to walk *up* to ABC from Base Camp at the start of our summit push. Heaven only knows how it can take the same time to walk *down*

1,200m as it took to walk up. I must be absolutely buggered.

One of the kitchen boys spots me approaching and runs out to meet me fifty yards short of camp with a kettle of hot orange juice. Although I'm keen to press on and reach camp, his gesture is kindly and the juice hits the spot. Then Dorje comes out with a *khata* scarf and a warm handshake. It must have been agonising for him to wait at Base Camp with his injury when he'd been intending to climb, but he looks genuinely pleased. I'm sure he is for his Sherpas, most of whom have never climbed Everest from the north before.

In the dining tent Phil turns up with three bottles of champagne to celebrate our success, but alcohol isn't what I need tonight. I feel like I'm in a daze, and find it difficult to share in the overall mood of jollity. Grant, who has proved to be in a different class to the rest of us, is drinking freely and very boisterous. He was a fantastic tent mate higher up the mountain, saying all the right things at all the right moments, but now his exuberance is the very opposite of what I need.

What I need is rest, to put me back to where I should be – mentally as well as physically. My mood surprises my teammates, and I know I must be coming across as dejected, unable to laugh at anything. This seems to be the way my body has responded to extreme mental exhaustion. Everything unnecessary has been shut down, and that includes my sense of humour. Hopefully tomorrow it will return.

For the others there is a mood of celebration. Even Mila the teetotaller treats herself to a glass of champagne. But there is also a more pensive note, summed up well by a comment Ian makes. Quietly confident and optimistic, he is the sort of person who just gets on with things without talking about them too much.

'I don't think I respected Everest enough before,' he says, 'but I do now.'

We're all very aware that we've needed a lot of help and good luck in order to achieve what we have. There will be people who say we haven't done anything particularly impressive, pointing out that we used fixed ropes and allowed Sherpas to do much of the hard work for us. This may be true, but it's also barely relevant. We're only seeking to stretch our own boundaries, not break new ground for the human race – it's not like any of us think climbing Everest makes us Reinhold Messner.

Meanwhile Margaret describes how she nearly died at Camp 3 trying to go for a pee in the vestibule of her tent. It was the morning after summit day, when the gale was howling outside. She had just lowered herself into position when an almighty gust bowled her over, dragging her underneath the doorway and down the hill. She was saved by Chedar, who was jerked awake by the roaring wind, and was doubtless surprised to open his eyes and see Margaret in a strange position, and on the verge of disappearing over the North Face. He leapt on top of her and began hauling her back into the safety of the tent. He needed the assistance of Nima Neru, lying the other side of him, to hold him steady and keep him from being dragged down himself.

It's clear my brain isn't functioning properly. Everything seems too surreal. I try to reflect on the last few days and bring everything into focus, but it's hard. I've made it to the top of the world and back down again safely. I didn't die of exhaustion, or fall off the Second Step or down a crevasse, or get frostbite. Or even get mauled by a yak. One of these days I expect it will sink in, but not yet. We have two days here at Base Camp to rest and pack, send emails and blog posts to let friends, family, and unknown supporters know we are safe, before jeeps arrive to take us back to Kathmandu.

But now it's time to head for my sleeping bag.

ACKNOWLEDGEMENTS

Thanks to the other members of my Everest team – Ian, Mark, Mila, Grant and Margaret – for being great company for six weeks.

Thanks to our amazing Sherpa crew – Ang Gelu, Chedar, Da Pasang, Dorje, Kami Neru, Nima Neru, Pasang Nima, Pasang Ongchu, and Pemba – without whom most of us would never have made it.

Special thanks to Chongba for being there when it mattered most.

Thanks to Phil Crampton for making it all happen.

Thanks to my editor, Alex Roddie, for his help polishing the text.

Most of all thanks to all of you, readers of my blog and diaries. I hope you have enjoyed this one, and I look forward to welcoming you back sometime. If you have not read it already then I hope you will enjoy my first full-length book, *Seven Steps from Snowdon to Everest*, about my ten-year journey from hill walker to Everest climber.

SEVEN STEPS FROM SNOWDON TO EVEREST

A hill walker's journey to the top of the world

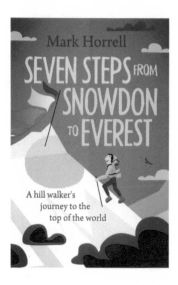

As he teetered on a narrow rock ledge a yak's bellow short of the stratosphere, with a rubber mask strapped to his face, a pair of mittens the size of a sealion's flippers, and a drop of two kilometres below him, it's fair to say Mark Horrell wasn't entirely happy with the situation he found himself in.

He was an ordinary hiker who had only read books about mountaineering, and little did he know when he signed up for an organised trek in Nepal with a group of elderly ladies that ten years later he would be attempting to climb the world's highest mountain.

But as he travelled across the Himalayas, Andes, Alps and

East Africa, following in the footsteps of the pioneers, he dreamed up a seven-point plan to gain the skills and experience which could turn a wild idea into reality.

Funny, incisive and heartfelt, his journey provides a refreshingly honest portrait of the joys and torments of a modern-day Everest climber.

First published in 2015. A list of bookstores can be found on Mark's website:

www.markhorrell.com/SnowdonToEverest

PHOTOGRAPHS

I hope you enjoyed the photos in this book. Thanks to the miracles of the internet you can view all the photos from my Everest expedition online via the photo-sharing website *Flickr*.

Everest North Ridge. Tibet, April/May 2012:
www.markhorrell.com/EverestNorthRidge

ABOUT THE AUTHOR

For five years Mark Horrell has written what has been described as one of the most credible Everest opinion blogs out there. He writes about trekking and mountaineering from the often silent perspective of the commercial client.

For over a decade he has been exploring the world's greater mountain ranges and keeping a diary of his travels. As a writer he strives to do for mountain history what Bill Bryson did for long-distance hiking.

Several of his expedition diaries are available as quick reads from the major online bookstores. His first full-length book, *Seven Steps from Snowdon to Everest*, about his ten-year journey from hill walker to Everest climber, was published in November 2015.

His favourite mountaineering book is *The Ascent of Rum Doodle* by W.E. Bowman.

ABOUT THIS SERIES

The *Footsteps on the Mountain Travel Diaries* are Mark's expedition journals. Quick reads, they are lightly edited versions of what he scribbles in his tent each evening after a day in the mountains.

For other titles in this series see Mark's website:
www.markhorrell.com/diaries

CONNECT

You can join Mark's **mailing list** to keep updated:
www.markhorrell.com/mailinglist

Website and blog: www.markhorrell.com
Twitter: @markhorrell
Facebook: www.facebook.com/footstepsonthemountain
Flickr: www.flickr.com/markhorrell
YouTube: www.youtube.com/markhorrell

DID YOU ENJOY THIS BOOK?

Thank you for buying and reading this book. Word-of-mouth is crucial for any author to be successful. If you enjoyed it then please consider leaving a review. Even if it's only a couple of sentences, it would be a great help and will be appreciated enormously.

Links to this book on the main online book stores can be found on Mark's website:

www.markhorrell.com/TheChomolungmaDiaries

18974817R00105